AINSLEY'S
MEDITERRANEAN
COOKBOOK

AINSLEY'S
MEDITERRANEAN
COOKBOOK

AINSLEY HARRIOTT

EBURY
PRESS

10 9 8 7 6 5 4 3 2 1

Ebury Press, an imprint of Ebury Publishing
20 Vauxhall Bridge Road, London SW1V 2SA

Ebury Press is part of the Penguin Random House
group of companies whose addresses can be found
at global.penguinrandomhouse.com

Penguin
Random House
UK

First published by Ebury Press in 2020

www.penguin.co.uk

A CIP catalogue record for this book is available
from the British Library

ISBN 978 1 529 10467 7

Project Editor: Lisa Pendreigh
Designers: Smith & Gilmour
Photographer: Dan Jones
Additional photography: Rob Partis
Home Economist: Claire Bassano
Food Stylist: Bianca Nice
Props Stylist: Tamzin Ferdinando

Colour origination by Altaimage, London
Printed and bound by Firmengruppe APPL,
aprinta druck, Wemding, Germany

Penguin Random House is committed to a sustainable
future for our business, our readers and our planet.
This book is made from Forest Stewardship Council®
certified paper.

INTRODUCTION

For my TV series, *Ainsley's Mediterranean Cookbook*, I went on a journey to explore the history of Mediterranean cooking and the routes the ingredients themselves have taken. My travels took me to the far corners of the Med and included cuisines from three different continents, taking in both the familiar and unfamiliar. Over the course of the journey, I discovered that – although the food of the Mediterranean is diverse, with each country having its own distinctive style – there are many similarities, both in cooking methods and ingredients. Olive oil is a prime example of this – each country producing a home-grown olive oil with uniquely different flavours. Bread is also at the heart of most Mediterranean meals and there is an enormous variety across the region – from rustic loaves and stuffed breads to a wonderful array of flatbreads.

The countries I visited are linked not only by the Mediterranean Sea, but also by the ancient spice routes. The almost land-locked Jordan was once linked to the sea via this trade and the spice routes played a huge role in shaping Mediterranean cuisines. Traders from North Africa and Europe travelled to the Middle East, bringing with them foods such as rice and chicken in exchange for spices from Asia. Invasions, colonisation and subsequent movement of people have also played a part in forming the cuisines around the Med. The Moors from the Maghreb, for example, heavily influenced Spanish cuisine by introducing saffron, almonds and various cooking techniques still popular today.

My first stop was the French island of Corsica and sailing around its coast by yacht was a wonderful way to take in the scenery. The island is stunning, with a rugged coastline and mountainous countryside. I must admit I knew very little about the food and what to expect. There's fantastic fresh fish, cooked simply with local herbs or in aromatic stews, but perhaps even better is the quality of the local meat. The island has a delicious selection of charcuterie, including dry-cured hams and smoked sausages. The Corsican countryside and shrubland, often referred to as the 'maquis', is a fragrant mix of herbs and flora with plenty of chestnut and fig trees. This fertile land flavours the meat, cheese, olive oil, wine and local honey of each region. Although their cuisine is influenced by France and perhaps more so by Italy, with their love of pasta and rich meat stews, Corsicans are fiercely independent – they have their own food traditions and live on what is available to them.

Up next was the short journey from Corsica to Sardinia, the second largest island in the Mediterranean. Seafood restaurants are plentiful and fish inevitably plays an important role in the region's cuisine. However, like Corsica, its real culinary delights lie inland in the countryside and mountains. There are more than four million sheep in Sardinia and lamb forms a major part of the local diet. Meats are cooked in a simple way, either over an open fire or slow cooked in stews. The traditional dish of suckling pig – *porcheddu* – is stuffed with herbs and fennel and roasted over juniper or myrtle wood. Although part of Italy, Sardinia is closer to North Africa and Corsica than it is to the Italian mainland and settlers have influenced the cuisine. The Spanish Catalan influence can be seen in the cuisine of the North and the Arabic influence can be seen in the island's unique pasta – *fregola* – which is shaped like couscous and often flavoured with saffron. Cheese is important to the island and pecorino and ricotta are among the island's exports.

My journey took me from Sardinia to Morocco – and it was quite a change to go from the midday riposa of Sardinia to the bustling souks of Marrakesh! The winding souks are a place to get lost in before joining the evening crowds in Jeema El-Fnaa Square for a bite to eat from the food stalls that seem to pop up from nowhere. Here, they sell everything: kebabs, tagines, snails and even sheep's heads. Morocco falls under the Maghreb region and its cuisine is one of the most diverse in the world, with influences from its interactions with other cultures. Probably the best-known food of the area is couscous. I happen to know a thing or two about couscous and enjoyed sampling a few new flavours on my trip. Spices are also commonplace in Moroccan cooking. I love their subtle way with spicing – nothing is too strong or hot. A touch of cinnamon and ginger delicately spicing a dish with a background hint of saffron is delightful! Slow-cooked stews such as the tangier or tagine (the name of the cooking dish rather than the stew) have been around for many years and each family has their own recipe. And, if you've been to Marrakesh, you'll know all about the tea – everywhere you go, a glass of mint tea is offered as a sign of hospitality.

Andalucía, in Southern Spain, was my next destination. The region's food is a vibrant fusion of Arabic and Spanish cuisines. At its heart are basic seasonal ingredients and olive oil, and the dishes are unpretentious and simply cooked. Fish and seafood are important to the local diet – fried and barbecued fish feature on most menus. The charcuterie of the region is outstanding – the famous Iberico pigs roam freely, eating the fallen acorns that give the meat its wonderful flavour, and smoky paprika-seasoned chorizo sausage is used in rice and fish dishes or served on its own as tapas. Tapas and *pinchos* (small snacks) come in endless forms, many of which have Arabic influences and are flavoured with cumin. It is said that the *tapa* was invented in Seville and this was my first stop in Spain. Tapas bars are everywhere in the city and nibbling your way through tasty local dishes is a great way to spend a couple of hours. I also stopped in Granada, a beautiful city with Islamic architecture and monumental churches surrounded by colourful street art. The first thing I did was go shopping for saffron in the Alcaicería market. The Spanish love saffron and use it freely – in paella, seafood dishes, desserts and cakes. I found that the people are so friendly in the region and have a relaxed approach to life – a siesta can only ever be a good thing!

My final stop, Jordan, might seem a little unexpected for a series about the Mediterranean, but I wanted to visit the region that had influenced the cuisine of the countries I'd already been to. The food in Andalucía and Morocco in particular would be very different today if their ancestors hadn't travelled the spice routes and participated in trade with India, Asia and the Middle East. The local food is mostly typical Levantine fare – you'll find mezze treats such as falafel, hummus, fattoush and tabbouleh, but it also has its own traditional delights. Labneh is strained yoghurt, almost like a cream cheese, that is served for breakfast or drizzled with olive oil and herbs to eat with bread. It's easy to make at home and I really recommend it. Lamb and veggie stews served with rice or grains are packed full of flavour and enhanced by the aromatic spices sumac and za'atar. A definite highlight was visiting Petra. Once a grand city built on the wealth generated by trade, it lay at the crossroads of many spice and trade routes. Today, the ancient city is a spectacle surrounded by mountains riddled with gorges and passages. It really is quite breathtaking.

I could talk much more about the wonderful cuisines of each country, the beautiful locations and welcoming people, but I'm sure you want to get cooking! I really hope you enjoy the recipes in this book and find a little of the unexpected along with the expected. Don't forget to turn up the music – perhaps a bit of flamenco – and have fun in the kitchen... Olé!

LIGHT BITES

CHARCUTERIE BOARD WITH HONEYED FIGS & CHILLI-GLAZED GRAPES

A charcuterie board or plate is a common offering in Corsica, Italy and France and is delightful as a sharing starter or light bite. Corsican meats are known as some of the best in the world and their charcuterie choice is exceptional – with *prisuttu*, *lonzu* and *coppa* (all dry-cured pork products) among the most prized. Figs are wonderful with cold meats and cheese and the island has an abundance of them, so they were a perfect choice for my charcuterie board. This is not a recipe as such, but rather a guide on how to build a fabulous dinner-worthy platter.

SERVES 4–6

80g fresh rocket
at least 6 slices each of
   a variety of charcuterie
   (prepared cured meats)
   of your choice
selection of cheeses,
   sliced (approx 150g
   of each cheese)
fresh crusty bread, to serve

For the Honeyed Figs
1 tbsp olive oil
25g butter
5–6 ripe figs, cut in half
1 tbsp runny honey
75g toasted hazelnuts,
   roughly chopped

For the Chilli-Glazed Grapes
2 tbsp runny honey
a pinch of chilli flakes
1–2 small bunches of
   grapes (red or green,
   or both – your choice)

For the dressing
1 tbsp balsamic vinegar
2 tbsp olive oil
1 tsp runny honey
salt and freshly ground
   black pepper, to taste

First, make the honeyed figs. Warm the oil in a frying pan over a medium heat. Add the butter and as soon as it has melted add the figs, cut-side down. Allow them to sizzle and cook for 2–3 minutes before turning and cooking the other side. Turn off the heat, drizzle over the honey and sprinkle over half of the chopped hazelnuts. Set aside.

Next, make the glaze for the grapes. Gently heat the honey in a small saucepan until hot, then add the chilli flakes and turn off the heat. Set aside.

To make the dressing, whisk all of the ingredients together in a small bowl, seasoning to taste.

Add 1 tablespoon of the dressing to a large mixing bowl and swirl around the sides. Add the rocket and use your hands to gently swirl the rocket to coat in the dressing (any remaining dressing can be stored in a jar in the fridge).

To serve, arrange the charcuterie, sliced cheeses, rocket and honeyed figs on a board or platter. Dip and swirl the grapes in the chilli glaze, allowing any excess to drain, then place on the board. Finish with a scattering of the remaining hazelnuts. Serve in the centre of the table with some fresh crusty bread for everyone to dig in.

CORSICAN MINT OMELETTE

Omelettes are so easy and perfect for a light lunch or a lazy brunch. Using fresh mint makes this a really fresh and vibrant omelette. In Corsica, they use olive oil rather than butter and the omelette is served flat rather than folded. Like their French neighbours, the Corsicans prefer a slightly runny centre, but you can cook yours all the way through if you prefer. When in season, *brocciu* (a ewe's milk cheese) is used in Corsica, but ricotta works just as well.

SERVES 1–2

100g brocciu or ricotta
    cheese
2 tbsp roughly chopped
    fresh mint leaves,
    plus extra for garnish
4 eggs
a pinch of dried chilli flakes
    (optional)
a pinch of herbes
    de Provence
1 tbsp extra-virgin olive oil
sea salt and freshly
    ground pepper

In a small bowl, mash the cheese with the mint and set aside.

In a separate bowl, beat the eggs with the chilli flakes, dried herbs and a good pinch of salt and pepper. Fold in the cheese and mint mixture until combined.

Heat the olive oil in a 20cm non-stick frying pan or omelette pan over a medium heat, then pour the egg mixture into the pan. As the eggs cook, quickly tip the mixture around the pan so that it cooks evenly. Continue to cook gently, lifting the sides to allow any runny egg to seep under (or you can place under a preheated grill for 1–2 minutes, if you prefer). When the top of the omelette is just set but the centre is still slightly runny, place a serving plate over the pan. Invert the pan, then lift it off revealing the omelette on the plate.

Serve, garnished with a few springs of mint.

MIDDLE-EASTERN SPICED BEEF PITTA POCKETS WITH YOGHURT DIP

Arayes are popular Middle-Eastern meat-filled pittas and it's easy to see why they are so loved – they are simple, quick and super delicious. The pittas are stuffed with subtly spiced meat and onions and then fried or baked until nice and crispy. If you want to spice things up, add a pinch of chilli flakes to the meat filling.

SERVES 4

250g minced beef or lamb
1 onion, grated
2 garlic cloves, grated
1 tomato, de-seeded
    and chopped
1 tbsp pomegranate
    molasses
1 tsp allspice
2 tbsp roughly chopped
    flat-leaf parsley
a good pinch of sea salt
a pinch of black pepper
4 pitta breads or flatbreads
2 tbsp olive oil, for brushing

For the Yoghurt Dip
250g thick Greek yoghurt
2 tsp tahini
a squeeze of fresh
    lemon juice
1 tbsp roughly chopped
    flat-leaf parsley

To serve
pickled chillies
    and gherkins
olives
fresh dates

Place the mince in a large mixing bowl and add the onion, garlic, tomato, molasses, allspice, parsley and salt and pepper. Mix well with your hands to combine all the ingredients.

Cut the breads in half and open out to form pockets. Fill each pocket with 1–2 heaped tablespoons of meat filling, using the back of a spoon to spread out the filling. Brush both sides of each filled pitta with olive oil.

Heat a frying pan over a medium heat. Cook the filled pittas in batches for 3–4 minutes on each side until golden brown and the filling is cooked through.

Alternatively, preheat the oven to 190°C/170°C fan/gas 5. Place the filled pittas on a baking sheet and bake for 15 minutes, turning them halfway through baking.

To make the yoghurt dip, mix the yoghurt with the tahini in a small mixing bowl, add a squeeze of lemon juice and stir in the parsley. Season to taste.

Serve the arayes hot, with the tahini yoghurt for spooning over and with a selection of pickles, olives and fresh dates on the side.

CHARRED SWEETCORN JACKETS WITH RAS EL HANOUT & LEMON BUTTER

Corn-on-the-cob has always been a favourite in my house and I'm always looking for new ways to cook it. Discovering all the spice blends in the souks of Marrakesh was a real eye- (and nostril-!) opener; I was fascinated by the amount of spices used in the ras el hanout blend. Don't worry about the husks of the corn getting charred; they are there to protect the kernels and your corn will remain lovely and succulent inside.

SERVES 4

4 corn cobs, with husks
150g butter, at room
    temperature
zest and juice of 1 lemon
1 red chilli, finely chopped
2 tsp ras el hanout
1 preserved lemon,
    finely chopped
2 tbsp chopped fresh
    flat-leaf parsley
a pinch of saffron
sea salt and freshly
    ground black pepper

Soak the corn cobs in their husks in a large bowl of salted water for at least 1 hour; this helps to prevent the husks burning on the barbecue.

Preheat the barbecue or a griddle pan over a medium–high heat.

In a bowl, mix the butter with the lemon zest and juice, chilli, ras el hanout, preserved lemon, parsley and saffron and season with salt and pepper. Beat together until well combined.

Remove any outer damaged leaves from the husks, leaving the healthy green ones intact. Carefully peel back the husks to expose the corn, leaving the husk intact at the base. Strip away any stringy silk threads exposed around the corn and discard.

Using your hands, rub the butter all over the surface of the corn, then roll back the husks to re-cover the corn and seal in the butter.

Place directly onto the hot barbecue grill or griddle pan. Cook for 18–20 minutes, turning occasionally.

To serve, just peel back the husks and enjoy.

LAYERED FLATBREADS WITH TOMATO SAUCE & POACHED EGGS

Pane Frattau is a simple, traditional Sardinian recipe using the local bread called *pane carasau* or *carta da musica* ('music paper bread'), so called because it is paper-thin like a sheet of music. When filming in Sardinia, I visited the family run Pau Bakery in Siniscola, where Claudio and his mum Francesca showed me how they make the amazingly thin bread. Over here, you can buy it in most supermarkets or Italian delis. This is an easy recipe full of Mediterranean flavour and great for a tasty brunch.

SERVES 4

2 tbsp extra-virgin olive oil
1 small onion, chopped
2 garlic cloves,
    finely chopped
600ml passata
500ml hot vegetable stock
a small handful of basil
    leaves, shredded
2 large round sheets of
    pane carasau, broken
    or cut into quarters
4 eggs
a splash of white
    wine vinegar
pecorino cheese, for grating
sea salt and freshly ground
    black pepper

Heat the oil in a deep heavy frying pan over a medium heat, add the onion and cook for 4–6 minutes until softened but not coloured. Add the garlic and cook for 30 seconds until fragrant, then add the passata. Simmer for 15–20 minutes, stirring occasionally. Halfway through cooking, add 2–3 tablespoons of the stock to loosen the sauce a little. Remove from the heat, add the basil and season with a pinch each of salt and pepper.

Add the remaining stock to a saucepan over a medium heat and gently bring to a simmer. Place two pieces of the pane carasau bread on a plate, pour over a little of the hot stock and let it soak in for 5 minutes. Repeat with the other bread sheets.

To poach the eggs, bring a pan of water to the boil and add the splash of vinegar. Turn off the heat. Break one egg into a cup and carefully lower into the water, then repeat with the other three eggs. Cover the pan with a lid and leave for 3 minutes. Once cooked, remove with a slotted spoon and drain on kitchen paper.

To serve, place one piece of the soaked bread on each of four serving plates, top each one with a little of the tomato sauce and place another sheet of bread on top. Add more tomato sauce, top with a poached egg, season with a little black pepper and grate over plenty of pecorino cheese.

CHARRED ORANGE & SPICED ALMOND SALAD

I love using oranges in a salad and I made this dish while visiting the stunning city of Seville, which is famous, of course, for its bitter Seville oranges. The spiced crunchy almonds are a wonderful contrast to the soft citrus and the salad makes a lovely light lunch or a side dish for chicken, duck or fish. This would also be great with some Serrano ham or Manchego cheese.

SERVES 4

3 large oranges
a handful of rocket
1 green chicory, leaves
    separated and washed

For the spiced almonds
2 tsp olive oil
60g whole blanched
    almonds
½ tsp ground cumin
½ tsp ground coriander
¼ tsp chilli powder
a pinch of sea salt
2 tsp runny honey

For the dressing
juice of ½ lemon
4 tbsp extra-virgin olive oil
1 tsp fresh thyme leaves
sea salt and freshly ground
    black pepper

To make the spiced almonds, heat the oil in a small frying pan over a medium heat. Add the almonds, shaking the pan to coat the nuts in the oil and cook for 1 minute. Add the spices and salt and stir, then drizzle over the honey and mix well. Cook for a further 3–4 minutes until the almonds are golden and well coated in the spice mix. Remove from the heat, tip onto a sheet of baking parchment and leave to cool.

Top and tail the oranges and remove the peel and pith by running the knife from top to bottom, removing the sections of peel until you are left with a whole orange. Slice each orange horizontally into four discs, reserving any juices in a bowl, then pat the slices dry with kitchen paper. Squeeze the skins over a bowl to extract any last juices and set aside.

Heat a non-stick frying pan over a medium heat until hot, then add the orange slices and quickly sear on both sides until they begin to char. Remove from the pan and set aside.

Make the dressing in the bowl with the reserved orange juice, adding the lemon juice, extra-virgin olive oil, thyme and seasoning. Whisk together until combined.

Drizzle the salad leaves with a little of the dressing and gently toss to coat.

To serve, arrange the chicory leaves around a platter, place the rocket on top and then arrange over the charred orange slices. Roughly chop the spiced almonds and scatter over the salad, drizzle over a little more dressing and serve.

MIGHTY PORK & CHARGRILLED PEPPER SANDWICH

A *bocadillo* is a Spanish warm sandwich. Many varieties are available throughout the country and this *Serranito de Lomo* hails from Seville. It contains more filling than a typical *bocadillo*: seared pork tenderloin, salty cured meat, fried green pepper and garlic mayo. This is no ordinary sandwich!

SERVES 4

4 green peppers, de-seeded and quartered
4 tbsp olive oil
600g pork tenderloin, cut into 12 medallions about 2.5cm thick
¼ tsp dried chilli flakes
1 garlic clove, grated
175g mayonnaise
4 large bread rolls (a crusty sub or baguette-style works best)
3 tomatoes, sliced
12 slices Serrano or Iberico ham
sea salt and freshly ground black pepper

Heat a griddle pan over a medium–high heat until hot. Rub the peppers with 2 tablespoons of the olive oil, then char the peppers on both sides until soft. Remove from the heat and set aside.

Place the pork medallions on a chopping board and use a rolling pin to bash and flatten them slightly. Season with salt and pepper and drizzle with the remaining 2 tablespoons of olive oil. Heat a frying pan over a medium heat until hot, then add the pork, sprinkle with chilli flakes and cook for 2–3 minutes on each side until golden and cooked through.

Meanwhile, combine the garlic and mayonnaise in a small bowl and season with salt and pepper, mixing well.

Slice the bread rolls lengthways and spread both sides with garlic mayonnaise. Build the sandwich by placing the chargrilled peppers on the bottom half of each bread roll, then the pork medallions (three pieces per sandwich), followed by sliced tomato and finally the cured ham. Top with the bread lids and serve.

CHARGRILLED VEGETABLE PLATTER WITH LABNEH & POMEGRANATE

One of the beauties of walking around Amman in Jordan is that you get the wonderful aroma of chargrilling. This recipe is inspired by the smell of the city and the abundance of amazing vegetables available. You can mix it up with any firm vegetable you like. Labneh is a soft creamy cheese made from yoghurt and is a staple throughout the Middle East. It's easy to make your own (see page 215) or you can use a thick Greek yoghurt instead.

SERVES 4

60ml extra-virgin olive oil
2 tsp sumac, plus extra
  for garnish
½ tsp dried chilli flakes
½ tsp ground cumin
2 tbsp pomegranate
  molasses, plus extra
  for garnish
1 large aubergine or 2 baby
  aubergines, cut into
  1-cm slices
1 small squash, de-seeded
  and cut into 1-cm slices
2 small courgettes, trimmed
  and cut lengthways into
  0.5–1-cm slices
2 red peppers, de-seeded
  and quartered
3 tbsp pine nuts
zest of 1 lemon
175g Homemade Labneh
  (see page 215)
3 tbsp finely shredded
  mint leaves
seeds of 1 pomegranate
sea salt and freshly ground
  black pepper
warm flatbreads, to serve

Preheat a cast-iron griddle pan, chargrill or barbecue to high.

In a large bowl, combine the olive oil, sumac, chilli flakes, cumin, pomegranate molasses and ½ teaspoon of salt. Stir until well combined, then add the sliced and quartered vegetables and gently coat in the flavoured oil.

Place the vegetables on the hot griddle pan and cook until slightly charred and softened. You will need to do this in batches, so start with the aubergine and squash as they will take a little longer to cook (2–3 minutes on each side). Remove from the pan and set aside to cool on a plate while you finish chargrilling the remaining vegetables. Set all aside to cool to room temperature.

Meanwhile, in a dry frying pan over a medium heat, toast the pine nuts until they are golden brown and fragrant. Keep an eye on them because they can easily burn.

Stir the lemon zest into the labneh.

When the vegetables have cooled, season with a little salt and pepper and arrange on a serving platter. Scatter with the toasted pine nuts. Top with the labneh, mint and pomegranates seeds and drizzle with a little extra olive oil and pomegranate molasses. Serve with warm flatbreads.

FATTOUSH SALAD

Fattoush is a fresh, crisp salad popular throughout the eastern Mediterranean. It's a great way to use up any leftover flatbreads or pitta and makes a crunchy side dish or satisfying lunch on its own. Each country has their own version of fattoush and I have tried and made a few on my travels. In Jordan I was shown how date molasses is made and I used some of the wonderful rich syrup to make this salad. It worked so well that I would recommend getting some if you can, or you can use pomegranate molasses if you prefer.

SERVES 4–6

2 large pitta breads
   or 1 large flatbread,
   cut into bite-size pieces
olive oil, for drizzling
1–2 romaine lettuce hearts,
   roughly chopped
½ small onion, diced
3 tomatoes, de-seeded
   and diced
1 cucumber, de-seeded
   and sliced
6–8 red radishes,
   trimmed and sliced
a large bunch of flat-leaf
   parsley, leaves picked
   and coarsely chopped
a small bunch mint,
   roughly chopped

For the dressing
4 tbsp olive oil
juice of 1 lemon
1 large garlic clove, grated
2 tsp sumac
1–2 tsp date molasses or
   1 tbsp pomegranate
   molasses
sea salt and freshly ground
   black pepper

Preheat the oven to 180°C/160°C fan/gas 4.

Place the pitta pieces on a baking tray, lightly drizzle with olive oil and toss to coat. Bake for 8–10 minutes or until slightly crisp and lightly golden. The idea is to dry out the bread without burning it. Remove and set aside to cool.

Place the lettuce, onion, tomatoes, cucumber, radishes and herbs in a large bowl and toss to combine.

To make the dressing, put all of the ingredients into a small bowl and season. Whisk until well combined and emulsified.

Just before serving, add the pitta croutons to the salad, drizzle over the dressing and toss to coat. Serve immediately.

HERBY SESAME FALAFELS WITH HUMMUS

Some say the best falafel are found in Jordan. I agree. We tried delicious falafel pittas from street-food vendors in Amman. These herby falafel, crispy on the outside but light and fluffy on the inside, are simple to make and delicious to eat. For a healthier version, spray the uncooked falafel lightly with oil and bake at 180°C/160°C fan/gas 4 for 15–20 minutes. For Jordanians, hummus is a staple food, often served for breakfast, lunch or dinner. You can use dried chickpeas, if you prefer – soaked overnight, rinsed, then boiled in fresh water with bicarbonate of soda for 30–35 minutes.

MAKES 18–20 FALAFEL

For the Herby Sesame Falafels

250g dried chickpeas, soaked overnight in water
½ onion, roughly chopped
2 garlic cloves, grated
½ tsp cayenne pepper
1 tsp ground coriander
1 tsp ground cumin
1 tsp sea salt
½ tsp freshly ground black pepper
juice of 1 lemon
1 tbsp chopped fresh coriander
2 tbsp chopped fresh flat-leaf parsley
2 tbsp olive oil
1 tbsp gram (chickpea) flour, or more as needed
50g sesame seeds
sunflower oil, for frying

For the Hummus

2 x 400g tins chickpeas
6 tbsp tahini
½ tsp ground cumin
juice of 1 lemon
2 large garlic cloves, grated
1 tsp sea salt
1–2 tbsp extra-virgin olive oil, plus extra to serve

To serve

5 black olives
1 tbsp chopped fresh flat-leaf parsley
a good pinch of sumac
4 pitta breads
mixed salad

First, make the hummus. Drain the tinned chickpeas and reserve some of their liquid. Place the chickpeas in a food processor and blitz to a coarse paste. With the machine still running, add the tahini, cumin, lemon juice, garlic, salt, 1 tablespoon of the olive oil and 2 tablespoons of the reserved liquid. Pulse to mix together. Add more of the olive oil and reserved liquid until you have a smooth and creamy mixture. Put into a dish and set aside.

Next, make the falafel. Drain the soaked chickpeas and place in a food processor with the onion, garlic, cayenne, coriander, cumin, salt and pepper. Blitz until chopped into a coarse paste, then add the lemon juice, fresh herbs and olive oil. Blitz until well combined, then scoop the mixture out into a bowl. Stir in the gram flour as needed – you are looking for a soft but not wet paste.

Using damp hands, roll 2 teaspoons of the mixture into a ball. Continue shaping the mixture into 18–20 balls (they can be fiddly, but will come together when squeezed – if the mixture feels wet, add a little gram flour; if too dry, then add a little oil). Transfer the balls to a tray, cover and chill in the fridge for 1 hour.

Put the sesame seeds on a plate. Roll each ball in the sesame seeds until coated.

Fill a large deep heavy-based saucepan with oil to a depth of 4cm and set over a medium heat. Test the oil is hot enough for deep-frying by dropping in a small piece of bread; it should sizzle and brown in 40 seconds – the oil should be hot, but not smoking. Add the falafels in batches of no more than 6 at a time and fry for 3–4 minutes, turning halfway through, until crisp and golden brown. Remove with a slotted spoon to drain on kitchen paper. Bring the oil back up to temperature before cooking the next batch, but make sure it doesn't get too hot as this makes the balls break apart.

To serve, make an indentation in the hummus with the back of a spoon and drizzle in extra-virgin olive oil. Garnish with olives, parsley and sumac. Serve the hot falafel with pitta and salad.

QUICK FLATBREADS WITH ROASTED TOMATO SALSA

When filming in Marrakesh, I had the pleasure of visiting Chez Lamine in what is known as Lamb Alley. Their lamb is roasted in the ground behind the restaurant until it is succulent and full of flavour. My flatbreads flavoured with peppery, oniony nigella seeds and my fresh tomato salsa were the perfect accompaniments to their delicious lamb. Serve with my Middle-Eastern Slow-Roasted Lamb (see page 175) or as part of a mezze.

SERVES 4

For the Roasted Tomato Salsa
5 large ripe vine tomatoes, cored
1 tsp cumin seeds
4 garlic cloves, roughly chopped
1 small onion
1 red chilli, finely chopped
3 tbsp olive oil
a handful each of fresh mint and coriander, roughly chopped
sea salt and freshly ground black pepper

For the Quick Flatbreads
200g self-raising flour, plus extra for dusting
1 tsp baking powder
200g natural yoghurt
1 tbsp nigella seeds, soaked in a little boiling water (just enough to cover them)
½ tsp sea salt
a drizzle of olive oil, for greasing

First, make the salsa. Char the tomatoes over an open flame until the skins blister and blacken. Alternatively, place them on a baking tray and cook under a hot grill for 5–10 minutes. Once cool enough to handle, remove the skins and discard – they should slip off easily. In a large bowl, use your hands to roughly crush the tomatoes.

Heat a dry frying pan over a low heat, add the cumin seeds and toast for about 1 minute, shaking the pan continuously, until fragrant and toasted. Tip into a pestle and mortar along with the garlic and a pinch of salt and crush together. Add the mixture to the bowl with the tomatoes, then grate the onion over the tomatoes. Finally, add the chopped chilli and mix well.

Heat the oil in a frying pan over a medium heat until it just begins to smoke. Pour immediately over the tomato mixture and stir well. Set aside.

To make the quick flatbreads, place the flour, baking powder, yoghurt, nigella seeds and salt into a mixing bowl and mix together to form a soft sticky dough.

Turn the dough out onto a lightly floured work surface, dust with a little more flour and knead gently for 30 seconds until you have a smooth dough. Divide into four equal pieces and roll each piece into a circle about 5mm thick.

Heat a non-stick frying pan over a high heat. Drizzle a little oil onto a piece of kitchen paper and wipe around the pan to lightly grease it. Cook each flatbread for 3–4 minutes on each side, until golden and flecked with brown patches, then remove from the pan and wrap in a clean tea towel to keep warm while you cook the remaining flatbreads. Wipe the pan with more oil as needed.

When ready to serve, add the fresh mint and coriander to the salsa and mix well. Serve the warm flatbreads with the salsa.

CHICKPEA, TOMATO & SPINACH TAPAS

Spinach with chickpeas, or *espinacas con garbanzos*, is a popular *tapas* dish throughout Southern Spain, particularly in Seville where you will find it on the menus in both tapas bars and top restaurants. The origins of this recipe can be traced back to North Africa and the simple ingredients are combined with smoky spices, chilli and garlic to create a dish that is rich in flavour.

SERVES 4
AS A TAPAS DISH OR SIDE

2 slices of day-old
    sourdough bread,
    crusts removed,
    torn into chunks
6 tbsp olive oil
1 onion, diced
3 garlic cloves, grated
1 tsp ground cumin
1 tsp sweet smoked paprika
½ tsp dried chilli flakes
2 large tomatoes,
    finely chopped
2 tbsp sherry or red
    wine vinegar
1 x 400g tin chickpeas,
    drained and rinsed
350g fresh baby
    spinach leaves
1 tbsp chopped fresh
    flat-leaf parsley
juice of ½ lemon
sea salt and freshly
    ground black pepper
lemon wedges,
    for squeezing

Heat a large deep frying pan over a medium–high heat. Coat the bread chunks in 2 tablespoons of the olive oil and add to the pan. Fry until golden brown, then remove and set aside.

Reduce the heat, add a further 2 tablespoons of olive oil to the pan, then add the onion and cook for 4–6 minutes until soft but not coloured. Add the garlic, cumin, paprika and chilli flakes and cook for a further 2 minutes, then add the tomatoes, stir well and season with salt and pepper.

Transfer the contents of the pan to a food processor or a large pestle and mortar. Reserving four chunks of the toasted bread for later, add the remaining bread along with the vinegar to the processor or mortar. Blitz or pound to a rough paste, adding a little water if needed.

Add the remaining 2 tablespoons of olive oil to the pan and add the chickpeas. Cook for 1 minute over a medium heat, then add the pounded tomato paste back to the pan and stir well. Bring to a simmer, then add the spinach and stir until it has wilted. Check the seasoning.

Spoon the chickpea mixture into a serving dish and crumble the reserved chunks of bread over the dish to give a crunchy crumb, sprinkle with parsley and squeeze over the lemon juice. Serve immediately with more lemon wedges for squeezing.

GARLIC & CHILLI PRAWNS

Gambas al Ajillo is a popular Spanish tapas dish, which also makes a great mid-week supper when served on toasted bread with a side-salad. It's delicious and so easy and quick to prepare. For a really authentic touch, add a splash of dry sherry when cooking.

**SERVES 4
AS A TAPAS DISH**

16 large raw king prawns, shell on
4 tbsp extra-virgin olive oil
4 garlic cloves, sliced
½ tsp hot/sweet smoked paprika
½ tsp dried chilli flakes
juice of ½ lemon
1 tbsp finely chopped fresh flat-leaf parsley
sea salt, for sprinkling
lemon wedges, to serve

Sprinkle the prawns with a little salt.

Heat the olive oil in a large frying pan over a medium–high heat. Add the prawns and cook for 1–2 minutes, then turn. Add the garlic, paprika and chilli and cook for a further 2 minutes. Squeeze over the lemon juice, then sprinkle over a little extra salt and the chopped parsley.

Serve immediately with extra lemon wedges for squeezing and plenty of napkins to wipe your fingers after peeling the prawns!

TOASTED BREAD WITH TOMATO & HAM

Bread, tomatoes and ham – simple everyday ingredients, yet so delicious when combined. The quality of your ingredients matter with this dish, so make sure you buy the best tomatoes you can – it really does make a difference. *Pan con Tomate y Jamón* is eaten for breakfast in Spain and it's only so good because the tomatoes are so good. Simple but fantastic!

SERVES 4
AS A TAPAS DISH

4 slices of rustic bread,
  such as sourdough
good-quality extra-virgin
  olive oil, for drizzling
3 large ripe tomatoes
1 large garlic clove,
  peeled and cut in half
4 slices of Iberico
  or Serrano ham
a few basil leaves,
  to garnish
flaky sea salt, to taste

Heat a griddle pan over a medium–high heat until hot. Drizzle the bread with a little olive oil and toast on the griddle on both sides until nicely golden. Alternatively, place the bread slices on a baking sheet and toast in the oven for 12–15 minutes at 160°C/140°C fan/gas 3 until crisp.

Cut the tomatoes in half and grate into a bowl, the skin should stay on the grater. If the tomatoes are too wet, tip into a sieve to strain off some of the liquid, then return to the bowl. Season with salt and drizzle with a little oil.

Rub the garlic on one side of each piece of toast and top with the tomatoes. The Spanish like to use just a thin layer of tomato, but feel free to add more. Top each with a slice of ham and garnish with basil.

FENNEL, PEAR & WALNUT SALAD WITH CRISPY PARMA HAM

This bright and crunchy salad is great for a light meal or starter and even works as a side dish for Italian roasts or pasta. I love the combination of the fresh anise notes of the fennel and crisp pear with the salty Parma ham and cheese.

SERVES 4 AS A STARTER OR 2 AS A MAIN

4–6 slices of Parma ham
1 large fennel bulb, tops trimmed, thinly sliced on a mandoline, fronds reserved for garnish
2 ripe pears, cored and thinly sliced (tossed in lemon juice to prevent discolouring)
60g walnuts, toasted and roughly chopped
60g wild rocket
40g Parmesan or pecorino cheese, shaved
sea salt and freshly ground black pepper

For the dressing
4 tbsp walnut oil
1 tbsp sherry vinegar or red wine vinegar
1 shallot, very finely chopped
2 tsp runny honey
sea salt and freshly ground black pepper

In a dry frying pan over a medium–high heat, fry the Parma ham slices, one or two at a time, until crisp. Set aside.

Put all of the ingredients for the dressing in a small bowl, season and whisk to combine.

Place the fennel and pear slices, walnuts and rocket into a large bowl and season. Lightly toss through half of the dressing.

Arrange the fennel salad on a plate and roughly break up the crisp Parma ham slices over the top. Finish with the Parmesan shavings and fennel fronds, drizzle with the remaining dressing and serve.

VEGAN SPANISH POTATO SCRAMBLE

This is my version of a popular Spanish tapas dish called 'poor man's potatoes' – *patatas a lo pobre*. Although it only contains a few basic ingredients and doesn't look particularly pretty, it tastes fantastic! I've added tofu and a hint of spice to turn this into a deliciously satisfying vegan main course that's great for a lazy brunch. You can now buy vegan chorizo in some supermarkets, so try adding a few slices for a spicy and smoky kick.

SERVES 4

4 tbsp good-quality extra-virgin olive oil, plus extra for drizzling
450g waxy potatoes (Charlotte or Anya work well), cut into 3-mm slices
1 large onion, halved and thinly sliced
225–250ml hot vegetable stock
1 red pepper, de-seeded and sliced
1 green pepper, de-seeded and sliced
2 large garlic cloves, thinly sliced
½ tsp ground turmeric
½ tsp sweet smoked paprika
1 x 380–400g block plain firm tofu, crumbled with a fork
½ tsp dried oregano
2–3 tbsp chopped fresh flat-leaf parsley
sea salt and freshly ground black pepper

Heat 2 tablespoons of the olive oil in a large deep-sided frying or sauté pan over a medium–high heat. Add the potatoes and onions and stir to coat in the oil, then season and cook for 4–5 minutes, turning the potatoes frequently to prevent burning, until brown in places. Reduce the heat to medium, add 225ml of the vegetable stock, then cover and cook for 8–10 minutes, or until the potatoes have softened, stirring occasionally to prevent sticking and adding a splash of extra stock if it looks as though it is drying out. Remove the mixture from the pan and set aside.

Use kitchen paper to wipe the frying pan of any remaining liquid, then add the remaining 2 tablespoons of olive oil. Add the peppers and cook over a low–medium heat for 4–6 minutes until starting to soften. Add the garlic and spices and stir through for 30 seconds until fragrant, then add the tofu and oregano. Stir everything together to combine and increase the heat to medium. Season well with salt and pepper and cook for a further 3–4 minutes. Add the potatoes and onions back to the pan, along with half of the parsley and drizzle with a little more oil if needed. Gently toss everything together and heat through for a further 3–4 minutes.

Serve scattered with the remaining fresh parsley and a grinding of fresh black pepper.

MOROCCAN VEGETABLE & SESAME SEED PARCELS

During our stay in Riad Monceau in Marrakesh, we were treated daily to a wonderful selection of appetizers, often including small pastries similar to these vegetable parcels – or *briouats*. Traditionally, a briouat is fried, but I've chosen to bake mine for a slightly healthier but equally tasty version.

MAKES 8–10

1 x pack of filo pastry
150ml olive oil, for brushing
2 tbsp sesame seeds

For the filling
2 tbsp olive oil
1 small onion,
    finely chopped
2 carrots, coarsely grated
1 courgette, coarsely grated
2 garlic cloves, grated
1 tsp ground paprika
2 tsp ground cumin
½ tsp sea salt
¼ tsp freshly ground
    black pepper
4 dried apricots,
    finely chopped
2 tbsp finely chopped
    fresh coriander

Preheat the oven to 200°C/180°C fan/gas 6.

First, prepare the filling. Heat the oil in a sauté pan or a deep frying pan over a medium heat, add the onion and cook for 4–6 minutes until softened but not coloured. Add the grated carrots, courgette and garlic and cook for around 5 minutes until softened and the vegetables have become dry. Add the paprika, cumin, salt and pepper, and stir well to combine. Transfer the mixture to a bowl and stir in the chopped apricots and coriander until combined.

Lay the filo pastry out on a clean work surface and cut each sheet lengthways into three long strips of equal width. Cover the pastry with a damp tea towel while you work so that it doesn't dry out. Lay out one strip of filo with the short side facing you, brush with oil, then place another sheet directly on top and brush with oil again. Place 1 tablespoon of the filling mixture in the centre at the top of the pastry strips. Treating the pair of pastry strips as a single piece, fold one of the top corners down to make a triangle shape, encasing the filling. Continue folding the pastry over, maintaining the triangle shape, all the way down to the bottom of the strip. Brush the parcel all over with oil and place on a baking tray. Repeat with the remaining filo sheets until all the filling has been used.

Sprinkle the parcels with sesame seeds and bake for 12–15 minutes or until the pastries are crispy and golden brown. These are best served warm.

VEGGIE
& VEGAN

CORSICAN BAKED CANNELLONI WITH MINT, CHARD & CRÈME FRAÎCHE

In Corsica, stuffed pasta dishes are very popular; ravioli and cannelloni in particular. Traditionally, the local cheese, *brocciu*, is used and it also differs from Italian cannelloni with the use of fresh mint and chard. I'm using ricotta and pecorino because they are easier to get hold of, but do use *brocciu* or Corsican tomme cheeses if you have them.

SERVES 4

275g chard, stems removed
1 tbsp chopped fresh
    flat-leaf parsley
2 tbsp chopped fresh mint
2 tbsp extra-virgin olive oil
1 onion, finely diced
1 garlic clove, grated
2 x 400g tins crushed
    tomatoes
½ tsp dried oregano
250g ricotta
a good pinch of ground
    nutmeg
zest of ½ lemon
170g pecorino or
    Parmesan, grated
2 eggs
400g crème fraîche
16 dried cannelloni tubes
    (about 220g)
sea salt and freshly
    ground black pepper
green salad, to serve

Preheat the oven to 200°C/180°C fan/gas 6.

Bring a large saucepan of salted water to the boil over a medium heat. Add the chard leaves and simmer for 2–3 minutes, then drain and refresh in cold water. Pat the leaves dry, then finely chop and put into a bowl. Add the fresh herbs, mix together and set aside.

Heat 1 tablespoon of the olive oil in a frying pan over a medium heat, add the onion and cook for 4–6 minutes until softened but not coloured. Add the garlic, tomatoes, oregano and season with salt and pepper. Gently cook for 12–15 minutes, stirring occasionally, then remove from the heat and set aside.

In a large bowl, combine the ricotta with the nutmeg, lemon zest, 125g of the pecorino, 1 egg, 100g of the crème fraîche and the remaining 1 tablespoon of olive oil. Mash together with a fork until smooth. Add the chard mixture, season with a little salt and a generous grinding of black pepper and stir everything together until well combined. Using a teaspoon, fill the cannelloni tubes with the mixture.

Pour a third of the tomato sauce into the bottom of a baking or lasagne dish (approx. 25 x 25cm). Place the filled cannelloni on top, then top with the remaining tomato sauce. Beat the remaining 300g crème fraîche with the remaining egg and pour on top of the tomato sauce. Scatter with the remaining 45g pecorino and season with salt and pepper.

Bake for 35–40 minutes until the pasta is tender and the top is golden. If the top starts to brown too quickly, cover with foil.

Leave to rest for a few minutes, then serve with a simple green salad.

BAMIA OKRA, TOMATO & GARLIC STEW

Okra and tomato is a popular combination throughout the Med and you can find various versions of this dish from Greece to Egypt to Lebanon. This recipe is based on a tasty stew I had in Jordan, where it is also sometimes cooked with lamb. It's a simple and healthy vegan one-pot that's great served with brown basmati or couscous. You can use frozen okra if you can't find fresh.

SERVES 4

4 large ripe vine tomatoes
2 tbsp olive oil
1 onion, finely chopped
750g small or baby okra, tops trimmed, washed and drained
4 large garlic cloves, grated
2 tsp allspice or Lebanese 7-spice mix
1 tsp ground cumin
½ tsp cayenne pepper
1 x 400g tin crushed or chopped tomatoes
1 tbsp tomato purée
2 tsp red pepper paste (optional)
juice of ½ lemon
1 tsp sugar
300ml hot vegetable stock, or more if needed
1 bay leaf
2 tbsp chopped fresh coriander or flat-leaf parsley
2 tsp pomegranate molasses (optional)
sea salt and freshly ground black pepper
brown basmati rice or couscous, to serve

Char the tomatoes over an open flame until the skins blister and blacken (alternatively place them on a baking tray and cook under a hot grill for 5–10 minutes). When cool enough to handle, remove and discard the skins, then crush the tomatoes into a bowl, discarding the tough cores.

Heat 1 tablespoon of the olive oil in a large deep frying pan or saucepan over a medium heat, add the onion and cook for 4–6 minutes until softened but not coloured. Add the okra and sauté for 3–4 minutes. Make a clear space in the pan and then add the garlic and spices and cook for 30 seconds until fragrant. Add the freshly crushed and tinned tomatoes, stir well and cook for a further 2–3 minutes, then add the tomato purée, red pepper paste (if using), lemon juice, sugar, stock and bay leaf. Cover the pan with the lid and simmer for 15 minutes, then remove the lid, season with ½ teaspoon each of salt and pepper. Reduce the heat, stir in half of the chopped fresh herbs and the pomegranate molasses (if using) and cook for a further 10–15 minutes, uncovered, until the okra is tender. If the mixture starts to look dry, add a little more stock as needed.

Serve hot over brown basmati rice or couscous, garnished with the remaining chopped herbs.

CARROT, COURGETTE & BROAD BEAN BAHARAT BURGERS

These tasty veggie burgers are full of flavour and texture. The Middle-Eastern spice baharat works perfectly with the vegetables and adds a delightful touch of smokiness. You can use chickpeas rather than broad beans, if you prefer. These are also great cooked on the barbecue!

**SERVES 4
(MAKES 8 SMALL OR
4 LARGE BURGERS)**

1 tbsp olive oil, plus
    extra for brushing
1 onion, finely chopped
1 tbsp baharat spice blend
½ tsp pul biber or dried
    chilli flakes (optional)
1 garlic clove, grated
225g carrots, coarsely
    grated
2 medium courgettes,
    coarsely grated and
    squeezed to remove
    excess moisture
1 x 400g tin broad beans,
    drained and rinsed
75g wholemeal
    breadcrumbs,
    or more if needed
zest of ½ lemon
2 tbsp crunchy peanut
    or cashew butter
1 egg yolk
2 tbsp finely chopped
    fresh flat-leaf parsley
1 tbsp finely chopped
    fresh coriander
sea salt and freshly
    ground black pepper

To serve
1 tbsp finely chopped
    fresh coriander
3 tbsp mayonnaise
4 sesame burger buns or
    pitta pockets, warmed
mixed salad leaves
sliced tomatoes

Heat the oil in a frying pan over a medium–high heat, add the onion and cook for 4–6 minutes until soft but not coloured. Stir in the baharat and pul biber and cook for 30 seconds until fragrant. Add the garlic, carrots and courgettes and cook for 4–5 minutes until soft, then remove from the heat and leave to cool slightly.

Blend the broad beans in a food processor until smooth. Scoop out into a large bowl and add the cooked vegetables, breadcrumbs, lemon zest, nut butter, egg yolk, parsley and coriander. Season generously with salt and pepper and mix well to combine.

Using damp hands, shape the mixture into 8 patties. If the mixture is too wet, add a few more breadcrumbs. Cover and chill for 1–2 hours or until required.

When ready to cook, brush the outside of the burgers with a little oil and place in a lightly oiled frying pan over a medium heat. Without moving them around, cook for 6–8 minutes on each side until golden, turning the heat down if they start to brown too quickly on the outside.

To serve, in a small bowl, mix the coriander into the mayonnaise and spread a little onto each burger bun or the inside of each pitta pocket. Fill with the burgers, salad and sliced tomatoes.

CHESTNUT, ROSEMARY & THYME RISOTTO

Much of the beautiful island of Corsica is mountainous and sparsely populated, and the dense shrubland consists of many wonderfully scented herbs, including rosemary, myrtle, thyme, sage, lavender and mint. I've chosen rosemary and thyme to accompany chestnuts, another Corsican favourite, in this creamy risotto. Although making a risotto takes a little time and attention, it's really worth having a go at this – it's simple, comforting and delicious.

SERVES 2–4

2 tbsp olive oil
60g unsalted butter
1 small red onion,
 finely chopped
1 garlic clove,
 finely chopped
200g Arborio risotto rice
70ml dry white wine
1 tsp chopped fresh
 rosemary leaves
1–2 tsp fresh thyme leaves,
 plus extra to garnish
750–850ml hot
 vegetable stock
180g pre-cooked chestnuts,
 roughly chopped (see tip)
1 tbsp chopped fresh
 flat-leaf parsley
80g vegetarian Italian
 hard cheese (if non-
 vegetarian, feel free to
 use Parmesan), grated
extra-virgin olive oil,
 for drizzling
sea salt and freshly
 ground black pepper

Heat the oil and half of the butter in a large deep frying pan over a medium heat. When the butter has melted, add the onion and cook for 3–4 minutes until just beginning to soften. Add the garlic and cook for 30 seconds until fragrant. Add the rice and toast, stirring, for 2–3 minutes until translucent, then pour in the wine and cook, stirring, until it has evaporated. Add the rosemary and thyme and season with pepper, then stir to combine. Add the stock, a little at a time, ensuring that the liquid is absorbed before adding any more. Stir through, continuing to cook and adding the stock little by little. After 10 minutes add the chestnuts and then continue to add the stock, cooking and stirring for a further 6–8 minutes. Check that the rice is cooked to your liking (it should retain some bite), then stir through the parsley.

Remove from the heat and stir through the remaining butter and half of the grated cheese. Check for seasoning – you shouldn't need much salt, if any, because of the cheese. Serve immediately, topped with a drizzle of extra-virgin olive oil, a sprinkle of fresh thyme and the remaining grated cheese.

TIP: If you have time, you can roast fresh chestnuts to add even more flavour to this dish. Cut a small hole in the skin of each chestnut and place on a baking tray with a pinch of salt. Roast for 25–30 minutes at 200°C/180°C fan/gas 6 until the skins have split.

CHEESE & WALNUT-STUFFED AUBERGINES

Aubergines à la Bonifacienne are plump juicy aubergines stuffed with cheese and are a speciality of the town of Bonifacio in Corsica. Full of the flavours of the Mediterranean, they're perfect for a light meal with a side salad or as a main course served with a simple tomato sauce (see page 22). Traditionally, the Corsicans use *brocciu* sheep's cheese, but a hard goats' cheese also works well. I've added walnuts to add a lovely texture and rich nutty flavour.

SERVES 4 AS A MAIN

4 aubergines
200ml milk
150g day-old white bread
200g crumbled brocciu or
    grated vegetarian Italian
    hard cheese, plus extra
    to serve
1 garlic clove,
    finely chopped
1 egg, beaten
a pinch of dried chilli flakes
50g walnuts, finely
    chopped, plus extra
    to serve
8 basil leaves, chopped,
    plus extra to serve
1 tsp herbes de Provence
    (or a mix of dried thyme
    and oregano)
zest of ½ lemon
2 tbsp olive oil, for cooking
sea salt and freshly
    ground black pepper
a drizzle of extra-virgin
    olive oil, to serve

Bring a large saucepan of water to a simmer over a medium heat, add the whole aubergines and cook for 10 minutes. Drain and set aside to cool.

Meanwhile, put the milk into a small bowl, add the bread and set aside to soak for 10 minutes.

When the aubergines are cool enough to handle, cut in half lengthways and carefully scoop out the flesh using a spoon, making sure you leave a 5mm depth of flesh still attached to the skin (this helps keep the aubergine intact). Lay each aubergine half onto kitchen paper, cut-side down, so that any moisture can be absorbed.

Drain the bread, squeezing gently to remove any excess liquid, then put into a large mixing bowl. Roughly chop the aubergine flesh and add to the bowl along with the cheese, garlic, beaten egg, dried chilli flakes, walnuts, basil, herbes de Provence and lemon zest. Season with salt and pepper and mix thoroughly with your hands to combine.

Drizzle the aubergine skins with a little of the olive oil and season with salt and pepper, then fill each half evenly with the stuffing mixture, packing it down well.

Heat the remaining olive oil in a large frying pan over a medium heat, then fry the aubergines, stuffed-side down, for 5–6 minutes. Do not move them during cooking. Using a spatula or fish slice, carefully flip over and fry for a further 4–5 minutes until golden brown. Alternatively, bake in the oven for 30 minutes at 180°C/160°C fan/gas 4.

Serve immediately, garnished with extra chopped basil leaves, walnuts and grated cheese, with a drizzle of extra-virgin olive oil.

COURGETTE, LEMON & PECORINO SPAGHETTI

With the addition of vibrant mint and pine nuts, this is an eastern Mediterranean twist on a classic Italian pasta dish. It's a light, fresh and speedy number for the middle of the week; ready in under 20 minutes and utterly delicious. If vegetarian, check that your pecorino is suitable or use a vegetarian Italian hard cheese instead.

SERVES 4

400g dried spaghetti
  or linguine
1 tbsp extra-virgin olive oil,
  plus extra for drizzling
2 large courgettes, coarsely
  grated and squeezed to
  remove excess moisture
½ tsp dried chilli flakes,
  or to taste
4 tbsp pine nuts, toasted
1 tsp dried mint
zest of 1 lemon
70g pecorino or vegetarian
  Italian hard cheese,
  grated
6 fresh mint sprigs,
  leaves picked
sea salt and freshly
  ground black pepper

Bring a large pan of salted water to the boil over a medium heat, add the spaghetti and cook according to the packet instructions until al dente.

Meanwhile, heat the oil in a large frying pan over a medium-high heat, add the courgettes and fry for 2–3 minutes, stirring occasionally to make sure that it doesn't clump together. Reduce the heat to medium, add the dried chilli flakes, pine nuts, dried mint and lemon zest and cook for a further 1–2 minutes. Season with salt and pepper (but be sparing with the salt, as the cheese is salty).

When the pasta is cooked, drain, leaving a little cooking water clinging to the pasta, and tip into the frying pan with the courgettes. Drizzle with a little extra olive oil and add a third of the cheese. Toss everything together over the heat for 30–40 seconds until combined and check the seasoning.

Serve immediately, sprinkled with the remaining cheese and scattered with the fresh mint.

SQUASH & SWEET POTATO TAGINE WITH LEMON & PISTACHIO COUSCOUS

Squash and sweet potato work beautifully with earthy, aromatic Moroccan spices and saffron. This is a quick tagine that makes for an easy, yet impressive vegan lunch or dinner. Feel free to mix up the veggies. The zesty couscous is simple to prepare and makes a perfect side to tagines and stews.

SERVES 4

For the tagine
2 tbsp olive oil
1 large onion, chopped
2 garlic cloves, sliced
2-cm piece of ginger,
    peeled and finely chopped
1 red pepper, de-seeded and
    cut into 1.5-cm pieces
2 tsp ground turmeric
2 tsp ground cumin
1 tsp ground coriander
a pinch of dried chilli flakes
1 cinnamon stick,
    broken in half
a pinch of saffron
500g butternut squash,
    peeled and cut into
    2.5-cm chunks
450g sweet potatoes, peeled
    and cut into 2.5-cm chunks
500ml vegetable stock
50g sultanas
a handful fresh coriander,
    chopped
a large handful of baby
    spinach leaves
sea salt and freshly
    ground black pepper

For the couscous
200g couscous
300ml hot vegetable stock
juice of 1 lemon
3 tbsp roughly chopped
    pistachio nuts
2 tbsp chopped fresh mint
2 tbsp chopped fresh
    coriander
a drizzle of extra-virgin
    olive oil (optional)
sea salt and freshly
    ground black pepper

First, prepare the tagine. Heat the oil in a deep heavy-based frying pan with a lid over a low–medium heat, add the onion and fry for 4–6 minutes until softened but not coloured. Add the garlic, ginger and pepper and cook for 2–3 minutes, then add the spices and cook for a further 2–3 minutes, stirring, until fragrant. Add the squash and sweet potato and stir well to coat in the spices. Pour in the stock, add the sultanas and season generously. Increase the heat to medium and bring to the boil, then cover the pan with the lid and simmer for 20 minutes or until the squash is tender. Stir through half of the coriander.

Meanwhile, make the couscous. Place the couscous in a bowl and pour over the hot vegetable stock or boiling water. Cover and leave for 5–10 minutes until all the liquid has been absorbed.

Fluff the couscous with a fork to separate the grains and let cool a little before stirring through the lemon juice, pistachios and fresh herbs. Season to taste and add a little extra-virgin olive oil, if needed.

Remove the lid from the tagine and scatter over the spinach leaves, cover and leave to wilt for 1 minute before stirring through.

Serve the tagine in warmed bowls with the couscous on the side, sprinkling both with the remaining coriander.

MARJORAM-ROASTED VEGETABLE, LENTIL & HALLOUMI BAKE

While I was in Corsica, I tried many delicious vegetarian dishes that were simply prepared yet full of flavour from fresh herbs and garlic. Marjoram is a versatile and aromatic herb that works beautifully with vegetables; it's similar in taste to oregano but with a milder sweeter flavour. This dish is easy to prepare for a mid-week dinner – just toss it all together in the one dish! For a creamy topping, serve with a little Greek yoghurt or hummus. This is great on its own or with my Quick Flatbreads (see page 34).

SERVES 4

2 courgettes, cut
   into 2-cm slices
1 red onion, cut into
   8 thin wedges
1 medium aubergine,
   cut into small cubes
2 red peppers, de-seeded
   and cut into chunks
1 red chilli, de-seeded
   and finely chopped
2 large garlic cloves,
   chopped
2 tbsp extra-virgin olive oil,
   plus extra for drizzling
2 tsp fresh marjoram leaves
   (or 1 tsp dried oregano)
1 x 400g tin lentils,
   drained and rinsed
1 tbsp balsamic vinegar
250g cherry tomatoes
1 x 250g block halloumi,
   thickly sliced
zest and juice of ½ lemon
8–10 basil leaves, shredded
   with a few reserved
   whole for garnish
sea salt and freshly
   ground black pepper

Preheat the oven to 200°C/180°C fan/gas 6.

Put the courgettes, onion, aubergine, red pepper, chilli and garlic into a large, shallow baking dish, drizzle with 1 tablespoon of the olive oil, season well, then scatter over half of the marjoram and toss together. Roast for 16–18 minutes.

Remove from the oven and toss through the lentils and balsamic vinegar, then stir in the cherry tomatoes and sit the halloumi slices on top. Drizzle with another 1 tablespoon of olive oil and sprinkle over the lemon zest and remaining marjoram. Roast for a further 16–18 minutes until the tomatoes start to blister and release their juices and the halloumi is golden around the edges. If you like, you can brown the halloumi a little more under a hot grill for 1–2 minutes after baking.

To serve, drizzle with a little oil, squeeze over the lemon juice and scatter with the fresh basil.

MEDITERRANEAN STUFFED PEPPERS & BEEF TOMATOES

Baked stuffed vegetables are a foodie highlight throughout the Mediterranean and you can find regional variations on the fillings; all of which are delicious. This is a satisfying and tasty vegan main with soft roasted vegetables filled with subtly spiced, herby rice and pine nuts – comfort food at its best.

SERVES 4-6

200g long-grain rice
500ml hot vegetable stock
4 large peppers
4 large beef tomatoes
2 tbsp olive oil, plus
    extra for drizzling
1 red onion, finely chopped
3 garlic cloves,
    finely chopped
2 tbsp tomato purée
1 small courgette,
    finely chopped
    or coarsely grated
½ tsp dried chilli flakes
½ tsp ground cinnamon
2 tsp dried oregano
2 tbsp chopped fresh mint
2 tbsp chopped fresh
    flat-leaf parsley
zest of 1 lemon
75g pine nuts, toasted
sea salt and freshly
    ground black pepper

To serve
salad
vegan Greek yoghurt
crusty bread

Put the rice into a medium saucepan along with 400ml of the stock and a pinch of salt and bring to the boil over a medium–high heat. Par-boil the rice for 8 minutes, then drain and set aside.

If needed, slice a very thin layer from the bottom of each pepper to make it easier to stand them upright, then cut the tops neatly from each pepper and set them aside to use later as lids. Remove the seeds and discard. Cut the tops from the tomatoes and set them aside likewise. Carefully remove the tomato flesh and seeds with a spoon, then chop up the flesh and set aside.

Arrange the hollowed-out peppers and tomatoes in a deep baking dish (approx. 30 x 25cm), making sure they fit snugly so they can't fall over but are not too squashed.

Preheat the oven to 180°C/160°C fan/gas 4.

Heat the olive oil in a large frying pan over a medium heat, add the onion and cook for 4–6 minutes until soft but not coloured. Add the garlic and cook for 30 seconds until fragrant, then add the tomato purée, courgette and tomato flesh, dried chilli flakes, cinnamon and oregano and cook for 5–6 minutes until softened. Add the rice, stir to combine and cook for 2–3 minutes. Remove from the heat and stir in the fresh herbs, lemon zest and toasted pine nuts. Season generously and stir well.

Spoon the rice mixture into the hollowed-out vegetables. Don't overfill or pack the vegetables because the rice will expand during cooking. Place the pepper and tomato lids on top and drizzle with olive oil. Pour the remaining 100ml of stock into the dish around the vegetables, cover with foil and bake for 1 hour, removing the foil after 45 minutes, until the rice and vegetables are cooked and tender.

Serve hot or warm, with salad, a spoonful of vegan Greek yoghurt and plenty of crusty bread.

MUJADARA SPICED RICE & LENTILS WITH CRISPY ONIONS

A spiced blend of rice, lentils and crispy fried onions is just as fantastic as it sounds! Great comfort food and delicious with a fried egg on top, mujadara is a popular dish throughout the Middle East and eastern Mediterranean and this is a slightly quicker version using a tin of cooked lentils. Without the fried egg, this is also great as a vegan main with Fattoush Salad (see page 30) or as a side dish to Bamia Okra, Garlic and Tomato Stew (see page 52).

SERVES 4-6

2 large onions, halved and thinly sliced
1 tbsp plain or gram (chickpea) flour
200ml sunflower or vegetable oil
1 tbsp cumin seeds, lightly crushed
2 tbsp olive oil
1 tsp allspice
½ tsp ground cinnamon
½ tsp ground turmeric
300g basmati rice, washed
1 x 400g tin green or brown lentils, drained and rinsed
500ml vegetable stock
3 tbsp chopped fresh coriander or flat-leaf parsley with a few extra sprigs for garnish
sea salt and freshly ground black pepper
fried eggs or dairy-free-yoghurt, to serve

Place the onions in a shallow bowl and sprinkle with the flour and a good pinch of salt. Mix well.

Heat the sunflower or vegetable oil in a heavy-based saucepan with a lid over a medium–high heat. When hot (test by dropping in a little piece of onion to see if it sizzles), add the onion, in batches if necessary, and fry for 6–8 minutes or until golden and crispy. Remove with a slotted spoon to drain on kitchen paper. Repeat with the remaining onion, adding more oil if needed.

Drain any remaining oil from the pan and wipe out the pan with kitchen paper (you can keep the onion oil for cooking curries or stews). Add the cumin seeds to the dry pan and toast over a medium heat for 1 minute until fragrant. Add the olive oil and, when hot, add the ground spices. Add the rice along with ¼ teaspoon of salt and a generous grinding of black pepper. Stir to coat the rice for 1–2 minutes, then add the lentils and stock. Bring to the boil, then cover the pan with the lid, reduce the heat to low and simmer gently for 15 minutes.

Remove from the heat, put a tea towel under the lid of the saucepan to stop any steam escaping and leave to sit, covered, for 8–10 minutes.

Meanwhile, fry the eggs (if using) to your liking.

Fluff the rice with a fork, check the seasoning, then add half of the fried onions and half the fresh herbs and fold through. Spoon the rice onto serving plates or bowls and top with a fried egg (or a dollop of dairy-free yoghurt), the remaining crispy onions and sprinkle over the remaining fresh herbs.

MINESTRONE WITH FREGOLA & HERB OIL

Minestrone is a classic hearty Italian soup featuring on all the menus in Sardinia. The North-African influence on Sardinian cuisine is shown in their love of fregola, a pasta grain similar to couscous. It's used in salads, soups and as a base for many pasta sauces and it adds a wonderful nutty texture to this soup. The secret to a good minestrone is to chop the vegetables all the same size so that they cook evenly.

SERVES 4

2 tbsp extra-virgin olive oil
1 onion, chopped
1 large carrot, chopped
1 fennel bulb, chopped
1 celery stick, chopped
100g fregola pasta
  or any small pasta
1 x 400g tin borlotti
  beans, drained
1 litre hot vegetable stock
1 rosemary sprig
100g green cabbage,
  shredded
3 ripe tomatoes, chopped
grated vegetarian Italian
  hard cheese, to serve

For the herb oil
a handful of basil leaves
a handful of spinach
3 tbsp olive oil
sea salt and freshly
  ground black pepper

Heat the oil in a large saucepan over a low–medium heat, then add the onion, carrot, fennel and celery. Sweat the vegetables for 12–15 minutes until softened. Don't rush this stage, cooking the vegetables slowly allows the sugars in the veg to release and gives the soup flavour. Add the pasta and beans and stir. Pour in the hot stock and add the rosemary, cabbage and tomatoes. Bring to the boil, then reduce the heat and cook at a gentle simmer for 15 minutes, stirring occasionally.

Meanwhile, make the herb oil. Blitz all of the ingredients together in a small blender. Season with salt and pepper.

Divide the soup between four warmed serving bowls, sprinkle with grated cheese and drizzle with the herb oil.

SUMMERY RICOTTA, COURGETTE, LEMON & MINT TART

The wonderful summery flavours of mint and lemon remind me of my time filming on the island of Corsica. The locals use fresh mint to flavour all sorts of dishes and they are particularly fond of pairing it with the local cheese, *brocciu*, which is similar in taste to ricotta. The fresh flavours of this savoury tart are perfect for a light lunch or picnic. It's also delicious with toasted pine nuts sprinkled on top.

SERVES 4–6

For the pastry
225g plain flour, plus extra for dusting
a pinch of table salt
110g cold unsalted butter, diced
3–5 tbsp cold water

For the filling
1 tbsp olive oil
3 banana shallots, thinly sliced
1 large courgette (approx. 200g), coarsely grated
5 large eggs
3 large egg yolks
200ml double cream
75g pecorino cheese, finely grated
a pinch of ground white pepper
75g ricotta
zest of 1 lemon
2 tbsp finely chopped fresh mint

First, make the pastry. Place the flour and salt into a bowl and mix well. Add the butter and rub in with your fingertips until the mixture resembles fine breadcrumbs. Gradually add the water a tablespoon at a time and mix in. When the pastry begins to come together, gently knead it into a smooth ball. Cover the pastry with clingfilm and chill in the fridge for at least 30 minutes.

Preheat the oven to 200°C/180°C fan/gas 6.

Unwrap the chilled pastry, place on a lightly floured work surface and roll out to about 3mm thick. Line a 25cm round loose-bottomed tart tin with the pastry, leaving a little excess hanging over the edge. Line the pastry case with a sheet of baking parchment and fill with baking beans or raw rice. Bake blind for 15–18 minutes, until the pastry is dry to the touch, then remove the parchment and baking beans and return the pastry case to the oven for a further 4–5 minutes until it is very lightly coloured. Use a sharp knife to trim away the excess pastry from the edge.

Reduce the oven temperature to 180°C/160°C fan/gas 4.

To make the filling, heat the oil in a frying pan over a medium heat, add the shallots and gently cook for 3–4 minutes until softened. Add the grated courgette and cook for 3–4 minutes until soft, then remove from the heat.

In a mixing bowl, beat the eggs and yolks with the double cream. Add the grated pecorino and a pinch of ground white pepper.

Tip the cooked shallots and courgette into the baked pastry case and spread out using the back of a spoon. Place heaped teaspoons of the ricotta randomly in the pastry case and scatter over the lemon zest and chopped mint. Carefully pour the egg mixture into the tart case. Bake in the oven for 35–40 minutes until the filling is set and golden.

Leave to cool in the tin for 5 minutes, then remove. Serve warm or cold with a fresh salad.

SHAWARMA TEMPEH FLATBREADS WITH CRUNCHY HARISSA CHICKPEAS

These vegan wraps are full of aromatic flavour. I'm using tempeh because it has an interesting nutty texture and taste that really works, but you can change to tofu if you prefer. For a healthier option, bake the tempeh in the hot oven for 25 minutes. Try spicing things up by adding some pickled chillies from a jar or drizzle over a little of my Hot Green Sauce (see page 136).

SERVES 4

For the Shawarma Tempeh
1 tsp ground cumin
1 tsp ground coriander
½ tsp cayenne pepper
½ tsp ground cardamom
½ tsp ground cinnamon
zest and juice of ½ lemon
2 garlic cloves, grated
3 tbsp olive oil
1 x 200g block of plain tempeh or tofu
sea salt and freshly ground black pepper

For the Garlic Sauce
250g non-dairy Greek-style yoghurt
2 garlic cloves, grated
½ tsp dried mint
a pinch of ground cumin
juice of ½ lemon, or to taste
sea salt

For the Crunchy Harissa Chickpeas
1 x 400g tin chickpeas
1 tbsp harissa paste
zest of ½ lemon
2 tsp olive oil
sea salt and freshly ground black pepper

To serve
4 large thin flatbreads
1 romaine lettuce, shredded
2 large tomatoes, sliced
½ red onion, finely sliced
2 tbsp chopped fresh coriander

First, make the shawarma tempeh. Place all of the spices, lemon zest and juice, garlic and 2 tablespoons of the olive oil into a bowl, season with salt and pepper and whisk together until combined. Cut the tempeh or tofu into strips or cubes, add to the bowl and leave to marinate for 1–2 hours or preferably longer, if you have the time.

Preheat the oven to 220°C/200°C fan/gas 7.

Next, make the garlic sauce. In a bowl, mix together the yoghurt, garlic, mint, cumin and add lemon juice to taste. Season with salt and chill until ready to serve.

To make the crunchy harissa chickpeas, place all of the ingredients except the seasoning in a large bowl and mix together until the chickpeas are well coated in the harissa. Tip into a baking tray, season with salt and pepper and roast for 18–20 minutes, giving the tray a shake halfway through the cooking time.

When the chickpeas are almost cooked, heat the remaining 1 tablespoon of oil in a frying pan over a medium–high heat, add the tempeh and stir fry for 6–8 minutes, turning occasionally, until cooked through and slightly crispy. Drain on kitchen paper.

To assemble the wraps, warm the flatbreads in a microwave for 15–20 seconds or place in the warm oven for 1 minute. Load each flatbread with some of the shredded lettuce, sliced tomatoes and onion. Divide the crunchy chickpeas and shawarma tempeh between the wraps, top with garlic sauce and sprinkle with fresh coriander to serve.

WALNUT, CARROT & SPINACH KUKU FRITTATA

From the Middle East, kuku is similar to an Italian frittata but with a higher ratio of herbs and other ingredients to egg. Baking powder is also used to make it light and fluffy. The textures and flavours in this satisfying dish are wonderful and it's great served hot or cold as a snack or main course. Perfect for picnics or lunch boxes.

SERVES 4–6 AS A MAIN OR 6–8 AS A LIGHT BITE

100g walnuts
6 eggs, lightly beaten
1 tbsp plain flour
1½ tsp baking powder
1 heaped tbsp Greek yoghurt, plus extra to serve
2 tbsp olive oil
5 spring onions, finely chopped
1 garlic clove, finely chopped
2 large carrots, grated
4 tbsp chopped fresh coriander
4 tbsp chopped fresh flat-leaf parsley
4 tbsp chopped fresh mint, plus extra to serve
20g barberries or cranberries, soaked in water for 5 minutes, then drained and chopped
1 tsp ground cumin
1 tsp ground turmeric
½ tsp ground cinnamon
70g baby spinach leaves, chopped
sea salt and freshly ground black pepper

Toast the walnuts in a dry frying pan over a medium heat until golden brown and lightly toasted. Keep an eye on them because you don't want them to burn. Remove from the heat and set aside to cool slightly before roughly chopping.

In a large bowl, mix together the eggs, flour, baking powder, yoghurt and ½ teaspoon each of salt and pepper, whisking until well combined.

Heat the oil in a deep 26cm non-stick frying pan over a medium heat, add the onions and cook for 2–3 minutes. Add the garlic and cook for 30 seconds until fragrant. Add the carrots, herbs, barberries, cumin, turmeric and cinnamon. Lightly season, stir well and cook for 4–5 minutes until soft. Add the chopped walnuts, then stir in the spinach little by little until wilted. Pour the egg mixture on top, reduce the heat to low and cook gently for 12–14 minutes until just set.

Meanwhile, preheat the grill to hot (optional).

Put the pan under the grill for 3–4 minutes until the frittata is cooked through and the top is golden and firm to touch.

Alternatively, invert the frittata onto a board and then slide back into the pan to cook the other side.

Run a spatula around the edge of the frittata to loosen, then slide it onto a plate. Cut into wedges and serve with Greek yoghurt or labneh (see page 215) and a sprinkling of fresh mint.

LENTIL & SWEET POTATO KOFTA WITH HERBY TAHINI SAUCE

These healthy, vegan, spiced Middle-Eastern kofta are so moreish and are great for a light lunch, either served in wraps or with Fattoush Salad (see page 30) or Tabbouleh (see page 157) on the side. Tahini is often served with kofta and falafel in Jordan and my Herby Tahini Sauce makes a great dipping or drizzling sauce.

MAKES 14–16 BALLS

400g sweet potato,
    chopped into chunks
1 x 400g tin lentils,
    drained and rinsed
2 garlic cloves, grated
20g breadcrumbs (1 slice
    of bread, crust removed)
2 spring onions,
    finely sliced
½ tsp pul biber or
    dried chilli flakes
1 tsp ground cumin
1 tsp sumac or zest
    of ½ lemon
1 tsp ground allspice
1 tbsp chopped fresh
    flat-leaf parsley
10 fresh mint leaves
25g pine nuts, toasted
1 tbsp gram (chickpea)
    flour (optional)
olive oil, for spraying
sea salt and freshly
    ground black pepper

**For the Herby
Tahini Sauce**
a small handful of
    fresh flat-leaf parsley
a small handful of
    fresh coriander
1 garlic clove, grated
a pinch of ground cumin
2 tbsp tahini
juice of ½ lemon
a pinch of sea salt

To serve
Fattoush Salad (see
    page 30) or Tabbouleh
    (see page 157)
flatbreads

Bring a saucepan of water to the boil over a medium–high heat, add the sweet potato and cook for 10–12 minutes until tender. Drain, leaving the potato in the colander for a few minutes to allow any moisture to steam off.

Place the cooked potato, lentils, garlic, breadcrumbs, spring onions, chilli, spices and herbs into a food processor. Pulse a few times until well combined but still with texture – you still want to see the lentils and small lumps of sweet potato. If you don't have a food processor, mash everything together with a fork or potato masher. Season generously, then stir through the pine nuts. If the mixture is too wet, add a little gram flour to help bring it together.

Using damp hands, divide the mixture equally and shape into 14–16 balls or patties (each about the size of a golf ball). Place on a plate or baking tray and chill in the fridge for 20–30 minutes.

Meanwhile, preheat the oven to 200°C/180°C fan/gas 6.

Remove the chilled kofta from the fridge, spray lightly with olive oil and bake in the oven for 25–30 minutes, turning occasionally, until golden and crispy all over.

To make the herby tahini sauce, put the herbs, garlic and cumin into a small food processor and pulse together until combined. Add the tahini and the lemon juice along with a good pinch of salt, and pulse to combine, then slowly blend in 40–60ml cold water until you have a smooth drizzling sauce. Set aside.

Serve the kofta with salad, flatbreads and a drizzle of the herby tahini sauce.

GRIDDLED ASPARAGUS & PEACH WITH GOATS' CHEESE & HAZELNUTS

Sweet peaches are fantastic in salads and chargrilling them elevates the flavour. Fruit and cheese is such a wonderful combination and this delicious salad is full of the fresh delights of the Mediterranean. Try adding some cooked grains, such as barley, if you fancy.

SERVES 4

150g goats' cheese, crumbled
3 tbsp full-fat Greek yoghurt
1 tbsp extra-virgin olive oil, plus extra for drizzling
zest and juice of ½ lemon
3 tbsp olive oil
2 tsp runny honey
4 fresh ripe peaches or nectarines, stoned and cut into wedges
125g asparagus tips
200g mixed baby salad leaves
a small handful of fresh mint leaves, roughly chopped
2 tsp sherry vinegar (or balsamic)
50g toasted hazelnuts, roughly chopped
sea salt and fresh ground black pepper

Place the goats' cheese into a food processor along with the yoghurt. Blend until smooth, then add the extra-virgin olive oil, lemon zest and season with salt and pepper. Pulse until the mixture is soft and fluffy. Alternatively, whip all of the ingredients together in a bowl. Cover and chill in the fridge until ready to serve.

In a large bowl, combine the olive oil and lemon juice with 1 teaspoon of the honey and season with salt and pepper. Add the peaches and asparagus tips to the bowl and toss to coat in the dressing. The peaches and asparagus can be removed with tongs in the next step and the leftover dressing reserved for later.

Brush a large griddle pan or frying pan with a drizzle of extra-virgin olive oil and heat over a medium–high heat until just beginning to smoke. Add the asparagus tips to the pan and chargrill for 3–5 minutes, turning occasionally, until lightly charred and just tender. Set aside and keep warm.

Next, place the peaches into the hot pan, flesh-side down, and cook for 2–3 minutes on each cut side, until charred.

Meanwhile, in a separate large bowl, toss together the salad leaves and mint.

Whisk the remaining teaspoon of honey and the vinegar into the reserved dressing, adding a drizzle of extra-virgin olive oil, if needed. Check for seasoning. Drizzle a little dressing over the salad leaves and toss to coat.

Place the salad leaves on a large serving platter and arrange the griddled asparagus and peaches on top. Scatter over the toasted hazelnuts and top with spoonfuls of the soft whipped goats' cheese. Drizzle with any remaining dressing, season with a good grind of black pepper and serve.

NUTTY PEARL COUSCOUS SALAD WITH FETA & DATES

Pearl couscous – Israeli couscous, giant couscous or ptitim, as it is variously known – is a small pasta with a nutty texture, and it carries flavours well. Dates are great in salads, being sticky, sweet and savoury all at the same time, and they also pair nicely with nuts. I tried some delicious nut-stuffed dates from a stall in Jemaa el-Fnaa square in Marrakesh. Medjool dates from Morocco are the sweetest variety and they have a chewy texture. This salad is fantastic on its own or as a side dish for a barbecue or picnic spread. It's also great the next day – make double the amount, take it to work and be the envy of your colleagues! Leave out the feta for a tasty vegan salad.

SERVES 4 AS A MAIN OR 6 AS A SIDE

250g pearl/giant couscous
extra-virgin olive oil,
    for drizzling
2 spring onions,
    finely sliced
1 large carrot, grated
40g pistachios,
    roughly chopped
35g pine nuts, toasted
25g walnuts, toasted
    and roughly chopped
a large handful of baby
    spinach leaves
6–8 dates (preferably
    Medjool), pitted and
    roughly chopped
3 tbsp chopped fresh
    mint, plus extra
    leaves for garnish
seeds from ½ pomegranate
80g feta, crumbled or
    chopped
sea salt, to taste

For the dressing
3 tbsp extra-virgin olive oil
zest and juice of ½ lemon
1 tsp date molasses or
    1 tbsp pomegranate
    molasses
½ tsp nigella seeds
½ tsp rosewater, or
    to taste (optional)
a small pinch of sea salt

Cook the couscous according to the packet instructions, making sure that you don't overcook it – it should still have some bite. Rinse the couscous with cold water and drain well. Fluff the grains with a fork and drizzle with a little oil so that they don't stick together, then put into a large bowl to cool completely.

When the couscous has cooled, add the spring onions, carrot, pistachios, pine nuts, walnuts, spinach, dates and chopped mint. Season with salt and toss to combine.

To make the dressing, add the extra-virgin olive oil, lemon zest and juice, date molasses, nigella seeds, rosewater (if using) and salt to a small bowl and whisk until well combined.

Pour three-quarters of the dressing into the couscous salad and toss to combine, then arrange the salad over a serving platter. Scatter over the pomegranate seeds and crumbled cheese, then garnish with mint leaves and drizzle with the remaining dressing.

PENNE WITH ARTICHOKES, PEPPERS, SPINACH & ALMONDS

This pasta dish has a Spanish twist with chargrilled artichokes and roasted red peppers combined with toasted almonds. It's a delightfully simple and tasty recipe using storecupboard ingredients and great for a mid-week supper. Use the best quality jarred artichokes you can find – the chargrilled ones in oil really do add extra flavour to the dish. If you aren't following a vegan diet, top with some grated vegetarian hard cheese.

SERVES 4

400g dried penne pasta
 or other short pasta
 of choice
1 x 175g jar chargrilled
 artichoke hearts in
 olive oil
2 garlic cloves,
 finely chopped
1 medium–hot red chilli,
 finely chopped
3 roasted red peppers
 from a jar, sliced
50g Spanish or Kalamata
 olives, pitted and halved
35g chopped almonds,
 lightly toasted
extra-virgin olive oil,
 for drizzling
100g baby spinach leaves
2 tbsp chopped fresh
 flat-leaf parsley,
 plus extra to garnish
zest from 1 lemon
sea salt and freshly
 ground black pepper
a handful of flaked
 almonds, lightly toasted,
 to garnish (optional)

Bring a large saucepan of salted water to a rolling boil, add the penne, stir once, then cook until al dente, according to the packet instructions.

Meanwhile, strain the olive oil from the jar of artichokes into a large frying pan, then cut the artichoke hearts into quarters and set aside. Set the frying pan over a medium heat. When the oil is hot, add the garlic and chilli and cook for 30 seconds until fragrant. Add the artichoke hearts to the pan along with the red pepper strips and olives, season with salt and pepper and stir to combine. Cook for 2–3 minutes to warm through, then stir through the almonds and a good drizzle of extra-virgin olive oil. Cook for 1 minute, then add the spinach to the pan, a handful at a time, and allow to just wilt down.

Drain the pasta, reserving a little of the cooking water. Add the pasta to the vegetables along with 2 tablespoons of the reserved cooking water, stirring to combine. Add the parsley and lemon zest and check for seasoning.

To serve, share the pasta among warmed pasta bowls, drizzle with a little extra olive oil, if needed, and scatter with the parsley and toasted flaked almonds, if using.

RACHIDA'S SPICED ROAST CAULIFLOWER & CHICKPEA CURRY

I really enjoyed cooking with chef Rachida at the riad in Marrakesh and this sumptuous vegan curry is inspired by her use of Moroccan flavours and spices. Roasting the cauliflower really brings out its nutty and buttery flavour, which is delicious with the warm spices. For a floral hint, try adding a teaspoon of rosewater with the almond milk; for a bit of crunch, you can add a few Crunchy Harissa Chickpeas (see page 78). Serve with basmati rice or flatbreads.

SERVES 4

80g cashew nuts
    (or blanched almonds)
1 medium head of
    cauliflower, separated
    into small florets
3–4 tbsp light olive oil
    or vegetable oil
2 tsp cumin seeds, crushed
1 large onion, chopped
3-cm piece of fresh root
    ginger, peeled and grated
2 garlic cloves,
    finely chopped
1 medium–hot red chilli,
    finely chopped
1 tsp ground cinnamon
1 tsp ground turmeric
½ tsp ground coriander
3 cardamom pods, husks
    removed, seeds crushed
    in a pestle and mortar
½ tsp cayenne pepper
1 x 400g tin chickpeas,
    drained and rinsed
1 tbsp date syrup
    (or agave syrup)
60g soft dried apricots,
    quartered
100ml vegetable stock
275ml almond milk,
    or more as needed
3 tbsp chopped fresh
    coriander
30g flaked almonds, toasted
sea salt and freshly ground
    black pepper
cooked basmati rice or
    flatbreads, to serve

Put the cashew nuts into a bowl, cover completely with boiling water and set aside to soak for 20 minutes.

Meanwhile, preheat the oven to 220°C/200°C fan/gas 7.

Drain the soaked nuts, put them into a food processor and pulse until finely chopped. With the motor running, slowly pour in 75–100ml cold water until you have a smooth and creamy paste. Set aside.

Spread the cauliflower florets out in an even layer on a baking tray, then drizzle with 1–2 tablespoons of the oil and scatter over the crushed cumin seeds. Season with salt and pepper and toss to coat. Roast for 20–25 minutes in the top of the oven until nicely roasted and tender, turning the florets over halfway through cooking.

Meanwhile, heat the remaining 2 tablespoons of oil in a deep frying pan or sauté pan over a medium heat. Add the onion and cook for 8–10 minutes until softened and starting to brown, then add the ginger, garlic and chilli and fry for 1–2 minutes until fragrant. Make a clear space in the pan, add the spices and cook for 1 minute, then stir them into the onion mixture. Add the chickpeas and season with salt and a generous amount of pepper, then add the cashew paste, date syrup, apricots and the stock and cook for 5 minutes. Add the almond milk, partially cover with a lid and simmer gently for 10–12 minutes, adding more almond milk if the mixture appears dry. Add the roasted cauliflower to the sauce, check the seasoning and cook for a final 2–3 minutes. Stir through half of the coriander.

Transfer the curry to a warm serving dish and scatter with the remaining coriander and toasted almond flakes. Serve with basmati rice or flatbreads on the side.

FISH & SEAFOOD

FISH STEW WITH SPICED GARLIC MAYO

Filming by the sea in Corsica and wondering what to cook… Fish, of course!
This is one of my favourite ways to eat fish, a traditional French dish
with a homemade spiced garlic mayo that is similar to a classic rouille.
Remember to buy sustainably sourced seafood and fish.

SERVES 4

4 tbsp olive oil
12 large raw prawns,
  peeled, reserving
  the heads and shells
200ml white wine
450ml hot fish stock
1 fennel bulb, sliced
1 onion, sliced
2 sticks celery, sliced
a pinch of saffron
2 garlic cloves, thinly sliced
2 tbsp tomato purée
200g ripe tomatoes,
  chopped
pared zest of 1 orange
1 bay leaf
350g non-oily fish
  (sea bass, bream, cod or
  haddock work well), skin
  on, cut into 3-cm chunks
sea salt and freshly
  ground black pepper

**For the Spiced
Garlic Mayo**
2 garlic cloves
a pinch of sea salt
2 egg yolks
1 tsp white wine vinegar
150ml olive oil
a squeeze of fresh
  lemon juice
a pinch of cayenne pepper

To serve
a handful of fresh flat-leaf
  parsley, chopped
slices of fresh bread,
  lightly toasted

Heat 2 tablespoons of the olive oil in a saucepan over a medium–high heat until hot, add the reserved prawn shells and heads and fry until they turn pink. Add the wine and cook until reduced by half, then add the stock. Reduce the heat and simmer for 5 minutes, then remove the pan from the heat and set aside.

Heat the remaining 2 tablespoons of oil in a separate large saucepan over a medium heat, then add the fennel, onion and celery and fry for 4–6 minutes until the vegetables are softened but not coloured. Add the saffron, garlic, tomato purée and chopped tomatoes, give it a good stir to combine all the ingredients and simmer for 10 minutes, stirring occasionally.

Meanwhile, make the spiced garlic mayo. Crush the garlic with the salt to make a paste, then transfer to a mixing bowl. Add the egg yolks and vinegar and use a balloon whisk to mix everything together. Slowly begin to add the oil, whisking continuously until the mixture begins to thicken. Once the oil is incorporated and you have a thick mayonnaise, season with lemon juice and a pinch of cayenne pepper. Set aside until ready to serve.

Stir the orange zest and bay leaf into the soup. Set a sieve over the pan and strain in the reserved stock. Stir, then bring to the boil and simmer for 8–10 minutes. Add the peeled prawns and chunks of fish and cook for a further 3–4 minutes until the fish is flaky and the prawns are pink. Taste and adjust the seasoning as required with a little salt and pepper.

Ladle the soup into warmed bowls and garnish with chopped parsley. Serve with the spiced garlic mayo and toasted bread on the side.

SEAFOOD SKEWERS WITH PEPERONATA

This is a real celebration of fish and it was the perfect light meal to cook on the boat in Corsica after a spot of paddle boarding. Simply cooked fish with a quick and tasty peperonata – delicious! *Pastis* is a French liquor flavoured with anise and its herby kick works so well with seafood. You can use any combination of fish and seafood you like for these skewers.

SERVES 4

4 tbsp olive oil
1 red onion, sliced
1 fat garlic clove,
    finely chopped
1 tsp dried oregano
1 red pepper, de-seeded
    and sliced
1 yellow pepper, de-seeded
    and sliced
a splash of pastis (such
    as Pernod or Ricard)
    or dry white wine
3 plum tomatoes,
    de-seeded and chopped
a pinch of sugar
1 lemon cut into 8 wedges
700g firm-fleshed fish,
    skinned and boned,
    cut into 16 chunks
16 raw king prawns, peeled
½ tsp chilli flakes
a handful of basil leaves
1 tbsp chopped fresh
    flat-leaf parsley
sea salt and freshly
    ground black pepper

Preheat a barbecue (if using to cook your skewers). If using wooden skewers, pre-soak them in cold water for 30 minutes before cooking.

Start with the peperonata. Heat 2 tablespoons of the olive oil in a frying pan over a medium heat, add the onion, garlic and oregano and cook for 4–6 minutes until softened. Stir in the peppers and cook for 3–4 minutes, then add the pastis and cook until the alcohol has burned off. Stir in the chopped tomatoes and sugar, and season with salt and pepper. Cover and cook for a further 3–4 minutes.

If not barbecuing, preheat a griddle pan over a medium heat.

To build your skewers, thread two wedges of lemon, four pieces of fish and four prawns onto each skewer, beginning and ending with the lemon wedges to help keep the fish in place. Drizzle a little oil over the skewers, then season with salt and pepper and a few chilli flakes.

Place the skewers onto the barbecue or griddle pan and cook for 3–4 minutes on each side until cooked through and the prawns are pink.

Just before serving, stir the basil into the peperonata.

Serve the skewers on the side of the peperonata, with a sprinkling of parsley on top.

GLAZED SUMAC SALMON WITH CHILLI-SPIKED COURGETTE SALAD

Salmon isn't a fish most commonly associated with the eastern Mediterranean, but it is a fish that can take a lot of flavour and spice. Zesty sumac works wonderfully with fish and here I've kept it simple so that the fish can shine. The light courgette salad with a little chilli kick is a perfect accompaniment.

SERVES 4

4 x 130g salmon fillets
1 tbsp olive oil, plus a little extra for greasing
1 tbsp pomegranate molasses, plus extra for drizzling
2 tsp sumac
1 tbsp chopped fresh coriander leaves (or micro coriander)
sea salt and freshly ground black pepper

For the salad
4 large courgettes, trimmed and cut into long strips
3 tbsp extra-virgin olive oil
1 medium–hot red chilli, de-seeded and finely chopped
juice of ½ lemon
2 tsp runny honey
8 fresh mint leaves, finely shredded
sea salt and freshly ground black pepper

Preheat the oven to 200°C/180°C fan/gas 6 and lightly oil a baking tray.

Place the salmon fillets on the prepared baking tray. In a small bowl, mix together the oil and pomegranate molasses, then brush the mixture over the top of the salmon fillets. Drizzle any remaining marinade over the fish, then coat the top of the fillets with a good sprinkling of the sumac. Season with salt and pepper. Bake for 10–12 minutes (depending on the thickness of your fillets), or until the fish is cooked through (the flesh will flake easily when cooked).

Meanwhile, make the salad. Put the courgettes into a bowl with 2 tablespoons of the extra-virgin olive oil. Season with salt and pepper and toss to coat.

Heat a griddle pan over a medium–high heat until hot, then griddle the courgettes, in batches, for 3–4 minutes on each side (depending on the thickness of your strips) until tender but still with some bite. Remove from the pan to drain on kitchen paper while you cook the rest.

In the same bowl used to toss the courgettes, mix together the fresh chilli, lemon juice, honey and remaining tablespoon of extra-virgin olive oil. Just before serving, add the griddled courgettes and shredded mint leaves and toss to coat. Check the seasoning.

To serve, divide the courgette salad between warmed plates and place the salmon fillets on the side. Drizzle over a little extra pomegranate molasses and scatter with chopped fresh coriander.

SEAFOOD PAELLA

Although paella originally hails from Valencia, over half of Spain's rice is grown in the area of Seville and all kinds of rice dishes are popular in the Andalucian region. You simply can't visit Spain without trying a traditional paella and I usually go for a seafood one. The subtle spicing of smoked paprika and saffron works so well with fish and seafood. Always cook a paella with a short-grain or round rice which absorbs liquid well, holds onto its starch and remains al dente. This dish is great for a dinner party and looks impressive served at the table for everyone to tuck in.

SERVES 4

500ml fish stock
a large pinch of saffron
5 tbsp olive oil
1 onion, thinly sliced
3 garlic cloves,
    finely chopped
1 red pepper, de-seeded
    and roughly chopped
200g ripe tomatoes,
    chopped
1 tsp hot/sweet smoked
    paprika
50ml dry white wine
200g Calasparra, Bomba
    or other short-grain rice
150g frozen peas
200g baby squid, cleaned
    and cut into thick rings
12 raw tiger (or king)
    prawns, peeled and
    de-veined
4 large raw tiger prawns,
    with shells left on
150g mussels, scrubbed
a handful of fresh flat-leaf
    parsley, chopped
1 lemon, cut into wedges

Warm the stock in a saucepan over a low heat and add the saffron. Remove from the heat and set aside to infuse for 5–10 minutes.

Heat the oil in a paella pan or wide deep frying pan over a medium–high heat, add the onion and fry for 6–8 minutes until soft and just beginning to turn golden. Add the garlic and pepper and cook gently for 4 minutes, taking care that the garlic doesn't burn. Stir in all the tomatoes and cook for 1 minute, then stir in the paprika and cook for 1 minute. Pour in the wine and let it bubble for 1 minute, then add the rice. Stir well until all the rice is coated with the wine and oil, then add the peas and the infused stock. Bring to the boil, then reduce the heat and simmer for 10 minutes without any further stirring.

Arrange the seafood on top of the rice, nestling the pieces down without disturbing the rice too much. Continue to cook, without stirring, for about 8 minutes. Keep an eye on the pan – if it begins to look too dry before the rice has cooked through, add a little hot stock or water. The finished dish shouldn't be wet: you are after a crunchy crust on the bottom.

Turn off the heat, then cover the pan with foil and leave to rest for 10 minutes.

Remove the foil and check that all the mussels are open (discard any that aren't). Garnish with the chopped parsley and serve with the lemon wedges for squeezing over.

CHERMOULA-SPICED FISH WITH CARROT RIBBON SALAD

I prepared this dish on the roof terrace of the Riad Monceau in Marrakesh and the fantastic smells from the barbecue drew quite a gathering, all wanting a taste of my chermoula-spiced fish. Make extra chermoula paste and store in the fridge to use for my Spicy Chermoula Fish Cakes (see page 111) or use to marinate chicken, vegetables or halloumi.

SERVES 2

2 whole sea bass
    (or similar), about
    225g each, gutted,
    scaled and cleaned
olive oil, for drizzling
    (optional)
lemon wedges or slices,
    to serve
a large handful of fresh
    coriander leaves, to serve

For the chermoula paste
1 tbsp ground cumin
1 tbsp paprika
a pinch of ground saffron
2 garlic cloves, thinly sliced
½ tsp dried chilli flakes
1 tsp cayenne pepper
juice of 1 lemon
a large handful of
    coriander leaves
2 large handfuls of
    flat-leaf parsley leaves
½ tsp freshly ground
    black pepper
½ tsp sea salt
3–4 tbsp extra-virgin
    olive oil

For the carrot salad
2 tbsp olive oil
1 tbsp freshly squeezed
    lemon juice
½ tsp nigella seeds
½ tsp ground cumin
a pinch of sea salt
2 large carrots, cleaned
    and cut into ribbons
    with a vegetable peeler
1 tbsp chopped fresh
    coriander leaves

Preheat a barbecue or the oven to 200°C/180°C fan/gas 6.

Place all of the ingredients for the chermoula into a food processor and pulse until a smooth paste is formed, adding more oil if needed. Check and adjust the seasoning if needed.

Use a sharp knife to score slits across the body of each fish. Reserving a little for basting, rub the chermoula paste all over each fish, making sure to include the cavities as well.

Put the fish into a fish rack and place on the hot barbecue. Cook for 10–12 minutes, depending on the size of the fish, turning halfway through and basting with the remaining chermoula. Make sure you don't overcook the fish – it is cooked when the flesh is opaque and easily flakes from the bone. Leave to rest for a few minutes before serving.

Alternatively, bake in the oven. Place each fish on a piece of greased foil or baking parchment, drizzle with a little extra olive oil and wrap loosely but securely, so that any juices or steam can't escape. Place on a baking sheet and bake for 12–15 minutes, depending on the size of the fish. To test whether it is cooked, cut a small hole in the package and test the fish with the tip of a knife – it is cooked when the flesh is opaque and easily flakes from the bone. Leave to rest for a few minutes before serving.

Meanwhile, make the carrot salad. In a small bowl, whisk together the olive oil, lemon juice, nigella seeds, cumin and salt. Place the carrot ribbons in a separate bowl. Just before serving, add the dressing and coriander to the carrots and toss well to combine.

Serve the fish alongside the carrot salad with lemon slices and scatter with extra coriander leaves.

MEDITERRANEAN SEA BASS & POTATO BAKE

We ate some beautiful baked fish on our journey around the Mediterranean. One of the most memorable was in Corsica – a whole baked fish served simply on a bed of potatoes and onions. Sometimes, it's the simplicity of dishes that make them taste so delicious; pared-back cooking really allows the ingredients to shine. This is also great with bream or snapper, or you can bake a whole fish on top of the potatoes for 18–20 minutes instead of using fillets. Try throwing in some capers, if you fancy.

SERVES 4

4 sea bass fillets, skin on
2 lemons: 1 thinly sliced;
    1 for squeezing
4 large waxy potatoes
    (Désirée work well),
    peeled and thinly sliced
1 red onion, thinly sliced
2 large tomatoes,
    thinly sliced
1 large garlic clove,
    finely chopped
2 tbsp olive oil
120ml white wine
2 bay leaves
3 thyme sprigs
3 tbsp chopped fresh
    flat-leaf parsley
2 tsp fresh marjoram
    or oregano leaves
sea salt and freshly
    ground black pepper
fresh bread, to serve

Preheat the oven to 200°C/180°C fan/gas 6. Line an ovenproof dish with baking parchment.

Season the fish fillets with salt and pepper and squeeze over a little lemon juice. Set aside.

Layer the potatoes and onions in the bottom of the lined ovenproof dish, season well with salt and black pepper, then add a layer of tomatoes. Sprinkle over the garlic, then place a few lemon slices on top. Drizzle over the oil, squeeze over some more lemon juice and pour in the wine. Add the bay leaves and thyme sprigs, 2 tablespoons of the parsley and sprinkle over half of the marjoram leaves. Season well with salt and pepper, cover with foil and bake for 25–30 minutes.

Remove the dish from the oven and lay the fish fillets in the dish skin-side up. Sprinkle with the remaining marjoram and bake uncovered for a further 12–14 minutes or until the fish is cooked through (it should flake easily when cooked).

Use a spatula or fish slice to carefully remove the fish from the dish, cover loosely with foil, and keep warm. Return the vegetables to the oven to bake for a further 4–5 minutes (if needed) until the potatoes turn golden brown in places.

Remove from the oven and serve immediately, scattered with the remaining fresh parsley, with some fresh bread on the side.

MOROCCAN FISH TAGINE WITH PRESERVED LEMONS

This tangy, quick, stove-top tagine is a healthy and delicious meal, perfect for a mid-week supper. Jarred preserved lemons are now easy to find in most supermarkets, but if you don't have any then use the zest and juice of one lemon. I've kept this mild but if you like things spicy, add a chopped red chilli with the garlic. Serve with couscous.

SERVES 4

a pinch of saffron
550ml hot fish stock
2 tbsp olive oil
1 onion, chopped
3 garlic cloves,
    finely chopped
1 tsp ground coriander
1 tsp ground cumin
½ tsp cayenne pepper
½ tsp ground cinnamon
600g small waxy potatoes,
    cut into wedges
3 ripe plum tomatoes,
    de-seeded and
    roughly chopped
2 tsp tomato purée
rind of 1 preserved lemon,
    roughly chopped
2 tsp runny honey
a large handful of
    green olives, pitted
2 tbsp chopped fresh
    coriander, plus extra
    to garnish
2 tbsp chopped fresh
    flat-leaf parsley
700g firm white fish fillets
    (such as sustainably
    sourced cod or haddock),
    cut into large chunks
sea salt and freshly
    ground black pepper
couscous, to serve

Add the saffron to the hot stock and set aside to infuse.

Heat the oil in a large casserole, tagine or lidded saucepan over a medium heat, add the onion and cook for 4–6 minutes until softened but not coloured. Add the garlic and cook for 30 seconds until fragrant. Make a clear space in the pan, add the spices and allow them to cook for 1 minute before stirring into the onions. Add the potato, tomatoes, tomato purée, preserved lemon, honey and the saffron-infused stock. Cover with the lid and simmer for 8–10 minutes until the potatoes have softened.

Check the seasoning and stir in the olives, fresh coriander and parsley. Add the fish, making sure the pieces are covered by the sauce, then season with salt and a generous amount of pepper. Cook, covered, over a low heat for 8–10 minutes or until the fish is cooked through (the flesh will flake easily when cooked).

Serve with couscous and scatter with extra fresh coriander.

SALMON EN CROÛTE WITH SPINACH, LEMON & CREAM CHEESE

Salmon en croûte may seem a little retro but it's also a little tasty! These easy fish parcels are a lovely main course for a dinner party because they look and taste fantastic and are really easy to prepare, allowing you more time to spend with guests. Tarragon is a French aromatic herb with a mild, sweet aniseed flavour that works beautifully with fish. Serve with either a simple green side salad, new potatoes and asparagus, or my Chilli-Spiked Courgette Salad (see page 98).

SERVES 4

olive oil, for frying
1 banana shallot,
    finely chopped
1 garlic clove, grated
60g baby spinach
    leaves, washed
a good pinch of
    ground nutmeg
100g cream cheese
zest of 1 lemon
1 tbsp chopped
    fresh tarragon
plain flour, for dusting
1 x 500g block puff pastry
4 x 175g salmon fillets
    (each 2.5cm thick),
    skinned and boned
1 egg, beaten
sea salt and freshly
    ground black pepper

Preheat the oven to 220°C/200°C fan/gas 7.

Heat a drizzle of olive oil in a frying pan over a medium heat, add the shallot and cook for 2–3 minutes until softened. Add the garlic and cook for 30 seconds until fragrant, then stir in the spinach until just wilted. Add the nutmeg and season with salt and pepper. Tip the mixture into a sieve and press firmly down on the spinach leaves to squeeze all the moisture out. Set aside to cool.

Put the cream cheese, lemon zest, tarragon and ½ teaspoon each of salt and pepper in a bowl and mash together.

On a lightly floured work surface, cut the pastry block into eight even-sized pieces and roll each out to a 23 x 15cm rectangle, trimming the edges if necessary. Place the salmon fillets in the centre of four of the rectangles and season with salt and pepper. Top each fish fillet with a quarter of the cream cheese mixture, gently spreading it to cover the fillets, then cover each one with a quarter of the spinach mixture.

Brush the edges of the pastry bases with a little beaten egg and lay a second sheet of pastry on top. Press down to seal and crimp the edges with a fork.

Place a non-stick baking sheet in the oven to heat up for a few minutes.

Meanwhile, make light slashes across each pastry parcel with a sharp knife, taking care not to cut right through, then brush the parcels with the remaining beaten egg. Put the parcels onto the heated baking sheet and bake for 25–30 minutes or until the pastry is cooked through and golden. Serve immediately.

SPICY CHERMOULA FISH CAKES WITH BEETROOT SALAD

When I had some leftover chermoula paste, I tried adding it to my favourite easy fish cake recipe and was so happy with the result that I had to share it with you. These oven-baked, gluten-free spicy fish cakes are great for a healthy lunch or supper.

**SERVES 4
(MAKES 8 FISH CAKES)**

450g floury potatoes, cubed
350g cod, hake or haddock fillets (or any sustainable white fish alternative)
2 tsp chermoula paste (store-bought or make your own, see page 103)
1 red chilli, finely chopped
1 tbsp chopped fresh coriander
oil spray, for greasing
sea salt and freshly ground black pepper

For the beetroot salad
1 tsp cumin seeds
1 tbsp freshly squeezed lemon juice
2 tbsp extra-virgin olive oil
1 tbsp chopped fresh flat-leaf parsley
1 tbsp chopped fresh coriander
1 x 250g pack cooked beetroot (not preserved in vinegar), chopped into 1-cm chunks
sea salt and freshly ground black pepper

To serve
a handful of watercress or rocket

Preheat the oven to 200°C/180°C fan/gas 6.

Place a large pan of salted water over a medium–high heat and bring to the boil. Add the potatoes and cook until tender. Drain and allow to steam dry for a few minutes before mashing.

Meanwhile, wrap the fish loosely in foil, place on a baking tray and bake for 15–20 minutes until the fish is cooked through. Remove from the oven, open up the foil parcel and allow to cool. Once cool enough to handle, flake the fish and remove any bones.

In a large bowl, mix together the mashed potatoes, flaked fish, chermoula paste, chilli and coriander and season with salt and pepper. Shape the mixture into eight even-sized round cakes.

Line another baking tray with baking parchment and spray with a little oil. Arrange the fish cakes on top, spray with a little more oil and bake for 25–30 minutes, until crisp and golden.

Meanwhile, toast the cumin seeds in a frying pan over a medium–high heat for 1 minute until fragrant, shaking the pan to prevent them burning. Remove from the heat and tip into a pestle and mortar, then lightly crush.

In a large bowl, mix together the lemon juice, olive oil, crushed cumin seeds, parsley and coriander, whisking until well combined. Season to taste, then add the beetroot and toss to coat.

Serve the warm fishcakes with the beetroot salad and salad leaves.

BAKED AROMATIC FISH PILAF

When I was in Jordan, I enjoyed a cook-along with chefs Mohammed Rabah and Raed Abu Zeineh at the Ayla Resort Golf Club, Aqaba. They made a wonderful Jordanian *sayadieh* – a traditional spiced rice-and-fish dish popular in many countries in the Middle East. This recipe is a quick and lightly spiced one-pan pilaf, inspired by their tasty dish. If you don't have any saffron, use turmeric to add a nice depth of flavour. Although this is a delicate dish, a drizzle of my Herby Tahini Sauce (see page 82) works really well.

SERVES 4

a pinch of saffron threads
600ml hot fish stock
2 tbsp olive oil, plus
　　extra for drizzling
1 onion, finely chopped
1 garlic clove, grated
1 heaped tsp baharat or
　　Lebanese 7-spice mix
½ tsp ground cumin
2 cardamom pods, husks
　　removed, seeds ground
　　in a pestle and mortar
300g basmati rice,
　　well rinsed
2 ripe plum or vine
　　tomatoes, de-seeded
　　and chopped
4 thick white fish fillets
　　(such as cod, haddock
　　or hake), skinless
　　and boneless
a pinch of dried chilli flakes
4 slices of lemon
2 tbsp pine nuts, toasted
2 tbsp chopped fresh
　　coriander
sea salt and freshly
　　ground black pepper

Preheat the oven to 200°C/180°C fan/gas 6.

Put the saffron threads into the hot stock to infuse.

Heat the oil in a large shallow casserole dish over a medium heat, add the onion and cook for 4–6 minutes until softened. Add the garlic, baharat, cumin and cardamom seeds and cook for 30 seconds until fragrant, then add the rice and gently fry, stirring, for 1 minute. Add the infused stock, season with salt and pepper and bring to the boil.

Scatter over the chopped tomatoes and add the fish fillets to the pan, nestling them into the rice. Sprinkle the fillets with the chilli flakes, season with salt and pepper, place a slice of lemon on top of each and drizzle with a little olive oil. Cover loosely with foil and place in the oven to bake for 10 minutes. Remove the foil, scatter over the pine nuts and cook, uncovered, for a further 3–6 minutes, depending on the thickness of your fillets, or until the fish is cooked through (the flesh will be opaque and will flake easily).

Serve scattered with coriander.

BAKED SARDINES WITH LEMON, ARTICHOKES & OLIVES

The word 'sardine' is said to have come from the island of Sardinia, where the fish were once found in abundance. Although not quite as common now, they are still eaten regularly, especially in the summer months. Baked sardines is a popular dish across the rest of the Mediterranean, too, which is no surprise really, as they're easy to prepare and taste fantastic. They're also pretty good for you – rich in omega-3 fatty acids, selenium and vitamin B12. Baking sardines in a quick marinade is a simple way to cook them and perfect for a light supper or lunch. Try with my crushed potatoes (see page 140).

SERVES 4

2 tbsp extra-virgin olive oil, plus extra for greasing and drizzling
1 lemon: ½ zested and juiced; ½ cut into thin slices
2 tbsp finely chopped fresh flat-leaf parsley, plus extra to serve
2 garlic cloves, finely chopped
½ red chilli, de-seeded and finely sliced into rings (or a good pinch of cayenne pepper)
2 tsp fresh oregano leaves (or 1 tsp dried)
1 tbsp capers, drained and chopped
½ tsp sea salt flakes
a pinch of freshly ground black pepper
8–12 sardines (depending on size), cleaned and trimmed, rinsed and patted dry
1 x 175g jar chargrilled artichokes in oil, drained and cut in half
a large handful of black olives, pitted
50ml dry white wine

To serve
lemon wedges
rocket salad
fresh crusty bread

Preheat the oven to 200°C/180°C fan/gas 6. Lightly oil a baking dish with extra-virgin olive oil.

In a large bowl, mix together the lemon zest and juice, parsley, garlic, chilli, oregano, capers, salt, pepper and the 2 tablespoons of olive oil. Add the sardines and gently toss until the fish are well coated inside and out.

Arrange the fish in one layer in the prepared baking dish and place the lemon slices and artichokes around the fish. Scatter over the olives and pour in the wine. Drizzle over any remaining marinade from the bowl and drizzle over a little more olive oil. Roast in the oven for 12–15 minutes or until cooked through.

Sprinkle with parsley and drizzle with a little more olive oil, then serve with lemon wedges for squeezing, a rocket salad and some fresh crusty bread.

DUKKAH CRUMBLE FISH PIE

Dukkah is a crunchy spice mix blended with toasted nuts and sesame seeds. Originally from Egypt, the spice has become popular throughout the Eastern Mediterranean and the Middle East. Here, it adds a wonderful crispy topping to an easy and classic fish pie. Dukkah can be kept in an airtight container for a couple of weeks and you can use it as an aromatic crunchy coating for fish, meat, veg or salad – try it sprinkled on a simple tomato salad (see page 170). It's also delicious mixed with a good olive oil and served as a dip for crusty bread or pitta. Serve with your favourite greens or peas.

SERVES 4

140g chunk of bread
  (seeded works well),
  torn into pieces
600ml full-fat milk
a pinch of saffron (optional)
1 bay leaf
700g mix of salmon and
  firm white fish (e.g. cod
  or pollack), skinned and
  boned, then cut into
  large pieces
75g butter, plus extra
  for greasing
30g plain flour
½ lemon, for squeezing
1 tbsp chopped fresh
  flat-leaf parsley
sea salt and freshly
  ground black pepper

For the dukkah

35g blanched almonds
20g hazelnuts
2 tbsp sesame seeds
2 tsp coriander seeds,
  lightly crushed
2 tsp cumin seeds,
  lightly crushed
½ tsp fennel seeds,
  lightly crushed
¼ tsp sweet smoked
  paprika
¼ tsp freshly ground
  black pepper
a good pinch of salt
a pinch of dried chilli
  flakes (optional)

First, make the dukkah. In a dry frying pan over a medium heat, gently toast the almonds and hazelnuts for 3–4 minutes, shaking the pan occasionally to toss the nuts. Tip into a food processor. Next, toast the sesame seeds with the coriander, cumin and fennel seeds for 1–2 minutes, then add them to the food processor with the nuts. Pulse a few times until the nuts are coarsely chopped. Add the paprika, pepper, salt and chilli (if using) and pulse once more to mix. You should have a coarse crunchy mixture rather than a paste, so don't blitz too much.

Tip the dukkah into a mixing bowl. Place the bread into the food processor and blitz until you have fine breadcrumbs. Add to the bowl with the dukkah and mix well, then set aside.

Preheat the oven to 200°C/180°C fan/gas 6.

Meanwhile, pour the milk into a deep frying pan, add the saffron and bay leaf, season with salt and pepper and slowly bring to the boil over a medium heat. Add the fish fillets, then reduce the heat and gently poach for 4–6 minutes. Use a slotted spoon to lift the fish onto a plate to cool slightly. When cool enough to handle, check for any stray bones, keeping the fish in large chunks. Strain the milk into a jug.

Melt half of the butter in a saucepan over a medium heat. Stir in the flour and cook, stirring, for 1 minute. Slowly pour in the infused milk, whisking constantly, then simmer over a low heat for 6–8 minutes, stirring occasionally until thickened. Stir in a squeeze of lemon juice, add the parsley and check for seasoning.

Lightly grease a deep ovenproof pie dish or medium lasagne dish with butter. Add the fish and spoon over the sauce to cover. Let rest for a few minutes to allow a slight skin to form, then sprinkle over the dukkah crumb and dot the surface of the crumb with the remaining butter.

Bake for 20–25 minutes or until the top is golden and the edges are bubbling. Serve immediately.

HOT-SMOKED SALMON WITH WILD RICE, ASPARAGUS & PEA SALAD

In Corsica, I was treated to a delicious yet simple meal of a smoked trout salad with fresh herbs. You can't get many of the Corsican herbs over here, so I'm using tarragon in my homage to that lovely salad. Tarragon is an important herb in French cooking and is often paired with fish or seafood. It has a unique aromatic taste similar to anise but sweeter. Hot-smoked salmon or trout is full of flavour and packs of fillets are readily available in supermarkets. This salad is also great with sliced avocado or wedges of soft-boiled egg.

SERVES 2

1 x 250g pack microwave wild rice, basmati rice or grains
100g asparagus tips or fine asparagus, ends trimmed
80–100g petits pois or young garden peas
extra-virgin olive oil, for drizzling
juice of ½ lemon
1 tbsp chopped fresh mint, plus extra leaves to serve
½ tsp nigella seeds or 1 tsp chopped chives
a large handful of pea shoots
a large handful of watercress
2 x fillets hot-smoked salmon or trout, skinned and flaked (or 100–125g ready-flaked)
sea salt and freshly ground black pepper

For the dressing
2 tbsp extra-virgin olive oil
4 tbsp crème fraîche
zest of ½ lemon
1–2 tsp Dijon mustard, according to taste
2 tsp finely chopped fresh tarragon leaves
½ lemon, for squeezing
sea salt and freshly ground black pepper

Cook the rice or grains according to the packet instructions. Tip into a bowl, fluff with a fork, season with salt and pepper and allow to cool to room temperature.

Meanwhile, bring a saucepan of water to the boil, add the asparagus tips and cook for 2 minutes, then add the peas and cook for a further 1–2 minutes until the asparagus is tender but still with bite. Drain and refresh under very cold running water. Transfer to a bowl, drizzle with extra-virgin olive oil, then squeeze over a little of the lemon juice to taste and season with a little salt. Set aside.

In a small bowl, make the dressing. Whisk together the extra-virgin olive oil with the crème fraîche, lemon zest and mustard and season well. Mix in the tarragon leaves and stir in a little lemon juice to taste. Loosen with a little cold water until you get a smooth, drizzling consistency.

Toss the mint and nigella seeds or chives through the cooled rice and squeeze in a little lemon juice to taste.

Arrange the salad leaves on a serving platter, spoon over the rice and arrange the vegetables and then the salmon or trout on top. Serve with the dressing drizzled over and a scattering of fresh mint leaves.

LINGUINE WITH ANCHOVIES & WALNUTS

Walnuts are used in both sweet and savoury dishes in Sardinia and they are so loved by the locals that there is even a yearly festival held in honour of their harvest. They are often used in pasta sauces in southern Italy and Sardinia and the earthy nut adds great flavour and texture. Don't be put off by anchovies – they melt down beautifully into the sauce, acting as a seasoning rather than imparting a strong fishy taste. Bottarga is a Sardinian speciality of dried and cured fish roe – it adds a salty and savoury note, which I think is quite special. However, it can be expensive, so this dish can be enjoyed without it, if you prefer.

SERVES 4

400g linguine or spaghetti
2 tbsp extra-virgin olive oil, plus extra for drizzling
2 garlic cloves, thinly sliced or grated
8–10 good-quality anchovy fillets in oil from a jar or tin, roughly chopped
80g walnuts, toasted and chopped
½–1 tsp dried chilli flakes
zest and juice of ½ lemon
2 tbsp finely chopped fresh flat-leaf parsley
sea salt and freshly ground black pepper
2 tbsp grated bottarga, to serve (optional)

Bring a large saucepan of salted water to the boil and cook the pasta until al dente, according to the packet instructions. Drain, reserving 3 tablespoons of the cooking water.

A few minutes before the pasta is cooked, heat the 2 tablespoons of oil in a large deep frying pan over a medium heat. Add the garlic and cook for 30 seconds until fragrant, then add the anchovies and cook for 1–2 minutes, crushing them with a wooden spoon to help break them down. Add the walnuts, chilli flakes and lemon juice and cook for 1 minute.

Tip the drained pasta into the frying pan along with the parsley and lemon zest and the reserved pasta water. Toss to coat in the sauce over the heat for 30–40 seconds, then season with black pepper and drizzle in a little more oil if required.

Serve immediately in warmed pasta bowls with grated bottarga on top (if using).

PAN-FRIED MACKEREL WITH SPINACH, GOLDEN RAISINS & PINE NUTS

Elegant enough for a dinner party, yet really easy to make, this fish dish is good to look at and even better to eat. Mackerel is a strong-flavoured fish and it works wonderfully with this slightly fruity, buttery and zesty combination of spinach, raisins and pine nuts, which is popular in the Catalan-influenced northern region of Sardinia. This dish also works well with sea bass fillets or halibut. Try with a side of potatoes or polenta.

SERVES 4

50g golden raisins
  or sultanas
4–8 fresh mackerel fillets
  (depending on size),
  skin on and pin-boned
1 tbsp unsalted butter
2 tbsp extra-virgin olive oil,
  plus extra for drizzling
50g pine nuts
3 garlic cloves, thinly sliced
a good splash of dry white
  wine (optional)
500g baby spinach
  leaves, rinsed
zest and juice of 1 lemon
olive oil, for frying
sea salt and freshly
  ground black pepper

Put the golden raisins in a bowl and cover with hot water. Leave to soak and plump up for 10–15 minutes, then drain well and set aside.

Season the fish fillets with salt and pepper and set aside.

Heat the butter and extra-virgin olive oil in a deep frying pan or sauté pan over a low–medium heat. When foaming, add the pine nuts and golden raisins and toast for 1–2 minutes, then add the garlic and cook for 30–60 seconds until fragrant. Add a splash of wine and cook for 1 minute to cook off the alcohol. Add the spinach (you may need to add a large handful at a time), lemon zest and a good pinch of salt. Increase the heat to medium and cook for 2–3 minutes, stirring, until the leaves are just wilted and coated in the garlic butter. Check the seasoning and turn off the heat, but leave the pan on the hob to keep warm while you cook the fish.

Place a separate large non-stick frying pan over a medium–high heat and add a small drizzle of olive oil. When hot, add the fish skin-side down. Reduce the heat to medium and fry the fish for 3 minutes until the skin is crisp and golden. Gently turn each fillet over and cook for a further 1–2 minutes, depending on the thickness of your fillets.

Arrange the spinach on serving plates and place the mackerel on top. Squeeze over the lemon juice to taste, season with pepper and drizzle with a little extra-virgin olive oil. Serve immediately.

PAPRIKA-BAKED HAKE WITH CHORIZO & WHITE BEANS

Chorizo, red pepper, tomatoes and beans is a popular combination in Andalucía, and this is a quick and easy fish dish with the vibrant flavours of the region. A white fish, such as hake or cod, is great for taking on the flavours of the smoky, spicy chorizo sausage. Serve with spinach or Tenderstem broccoli.

SERVES 4

3 tbsp good-quality extra-virgin olive oil
2 tsp sweet/hot smoked paprika
juice of ½ lemon
4 x 150g sustainable hake, haddock or cod fillets, skinned and boned
2 shallots, finely chopped
175g cooking chorizo, skinned and diced
1 red pepper, de-seeded and diced
2 large garlic cloves, finely chopped
50ml sherry or white wine
4 large ripe vine or plum tomatoes, roughly chopped
2 x 400g tins white beans (cannellini or butter), drained and rinsed
2 tbsp chopped fresh flat-leaf parsley, plus extra to serve
sea salt and freshly ground black pepper

Preheat the oven to 200°C/180°C fan/gas 6.

In a small bowl, mix together 1 tablespoon of the olive oil with 1 teaspoon of the paprika and the lemon juice to make a marinade. Put the hake onto a non-stick baking tray and brush with the marinade, then season with salt and pepper (reserve any leftover marinade). Roast in the oven for 10–12 minutes, depending on the thickness of your fillets, or until the fish is cooked (the flesh will be opaque and will flake easily).

Meanwhile, heat 1 tablespoon of the oil in a large frying pan over a medium heat, add the shallots and cook for 2–3 minutes until softened but not coloured. Add the chorizo and cook for 2 minutes, then add the red pepper, garlic, any remaining marinade and the remaining 1 teaspoon of paprika. Stir everything together and cook for 3–4 minutes. Add the sherry and cook for 1 minute to burn off the alcohol, then stir in the tomatoes and beans, season and simmer for 6–8 minutes. Stir in the remaining 1 tablespoon of oil and the parsley.

Share the beans among warmed serving bowls and serve with the roasted hake on top, garnished with extra parsley.

SALT-COD FISH BALLS WITH CHERRY TOMATO SAUCE

Here's a lovely dish to win you over if you're not already a big fan of salted cod. These Spanish salt-cod balls or *albondigas* are light, delicate, soft and creamy… Yum, a real winner! Salt cod (*bacalao*) is a staple in Andalucía – when I was in Seville and Granada, I enjoyed a wonderful variety of bacalao tapas. Salt fish is also really good value and you can buy packs of prepared fillets or *bacalao* in tins if you want to save time. Try it – you'll love it.

SERVES 4

For the Salt-Cod Fish Balls
250g salt fish or ready-to-use salt cod
150g fresh breadcrumbs
1 large egg, lightly beaten
2 garlic cloves, grated
3 tbsp finely chopped fresh flat-leaf parsley
4 tbsp plain flour
2 tbsp olive oil, or more as needed
freshly ground black pepper

For the Cherry Tomato Sauce
4 tbsp extra-virgin olive oil
1 onion, finely chopped
a splash of sherry or white wine
2 ripe plum tomatoes, roughly chopped
2 tsp sweet smoked paprika
100ml hot vegetable stock
½ tsp granulated sugar
1 x 400g tin cherry tomatoes
1 tbsp chopped fresh flat-leaf parsley, plus extra to serve
sea salt and freshly ground black pepper

To serve
fresh crusty bread
lemon wedges, for squeezing

If preparing your own salt fish, place the fillets in cold water and soak overnight, changing the water a couple of times, then drain.

Bring a large saucepan of water to the boil, add the salt cod and simmer for 10–15 minutes, depending on the thickness of your fillets. Drain well and pat dry. While the fish is still warm, flake and remove the skin and bones. Set aside.

To make the salsa, heat 1 tablespoon of the extra-virgin olive oil in a deep frying pan or sauté pan over a medium heat, add the onion and cook for 4–6 minutes until softened but not coloured. Add a good splash of sherry and cook off the alcohol for 1 minute, then add the plum tomatoes and paprika and cook for 4–5 minutes until the tomatoes soften. Stir in the stock, sugar and tinned cherry tomatoes and season to taste. Stir in the parsley and the remaining 3 tablespoons of oil and cook for 6–8 minutes. Keep warm.

Meanwhile, make the fish balls. Put the breadcrumbs into a bowl, add the flaked salt cod and mix well. Add the egg, garlic and parsley and season with plenty of black pepper. Mix well with a fork. Using your hands, squeeze the mixture together and form a ball. Divide into 16 equal pieces and roll each piece into a ball. Put the flour onto a plate and roll the balls through the flour to lightly coat.

Heat 2 tablespoons of olive oil in a deep frying pan over a medium heat. When hot, add the balls and fry for 5–6 minutes until golden brown all over, but still soft and moist inside. You may need to do this in batches, adding a little more oil if needed. Once browned, carefully remove from the oil with a slotted spoon and finish off in the tomato sauce for 1–2 minutes or serve tapas style with the sauce on the side.

Scatter the fish balls with fresh parsley. Serve with some fresh bread and lemon wedges for squeezing.

MEAT & POULTRY

BEST-EVER BEEF & RED WINE STEW WITH OLIVE & THYME DUMPLINGS

Sardinians enjoy rich stews made with wild boar, rabbit, beef or veal. This is my take on a hearty Sardinian red wine stew and I've added some fluffy dumplings to make it even more comforting. Cannonau wine is a full-bodied Sardinian red, often paired with beef because of its robust flavour. If you can't find it, a good-quality Italian red will do. Serve with cavolo nero or kale.

SERVES 4–6

2 garlic cloves, chopped
2 tsp fresh thyme leaves
a splash of red wine vinegar
300ml Cannonau red wine
zest of 1 lemon
850g beef stewing steak, cut into 3-cm cubes
4 tbsp plain flour, seasoned
3 tbsp extra-virgin olive oil
100g pancetta or smoked bacon, roughly chopped
2 red onions, chopped
2 garlic cloves, finely chopped
400–600ml hot beef stock, as needed
1 tbsp sun-dried tomato or tomato purée
1 bay leaf
1 rosemary sprig
2 carrots, halved lengthways and cut into chunks
2 tbsp chopped fresh flat-leaf parsley
sea salt and freshly ground black pepper

For the Olive and Thyme Dumplings
125g self-raising flour
50g butter, at room temperature
a pinch of salt and freshly ground black pepper
1 tsp dried thyme
50g green olives, pitted and finely chopped

In a bowl, mix together the garlic, thyme, vinegar, red wine, lemon zest and ½ teaspoon of freshly ground black pepper. Add the beef and stir to combine. Cover and marinate in the fridge for 1–2 hours.

Remove the meat from the fridge at least 30 minutes before cooking so it can return to room temperature. Remove the meat from the marinade and pat dry, reserving the marinade. Place the flour in a large bowl and add the meat pieces, tossing to lightly coat.

Heat the oil in a large, heavy-based saucepan or casserole over a medium–high heat. Add the meat in batches and fry for 6–8 minutes until browned on all sides. Remove the meat from the pan and set aside. Add the pancetta to the pan and cook for 2 minutes, scraping any remnants from the base of the pan. Add the onion and cook for 4–6 minutes until softened, then add the garlic and cook for 30 seconds until fragrant. Return the beef to the pan and pour over the reserved marinade and 400ml of the stock. Add the tomato purée, bay leaf and rosemary and bring to the boil. Cook uncovered for 10–15 minutes until the liquid has reduced by about a third. Reduce the heat, cover and simmer gently for 1¼ hours (checking occasionally to ensure that the meat is still covered by liquid; if not add a little more stock).

Meanwhile, make the dumplings. Sift the flour into a bowl and rub in the butter using your fingertips. Mix in the salt, pepper, thyme and olives and add just enough cold water to bring the mixture together into a dough. Roll into eight small dumplings.

Check the stew for seasoning and adjust according to taste. Stir in the carrots and half the parsley and then settle the dumplings on top of the stew, making sure that half of each dumpling sits just below the level of the liquid. Cover and cook for a further 25–30 minutes or until the meat is tender. If you like your dumplings with a golden top, put the stew under a hot grill for a few minutes to brown them.

Leave to rest with the lid on for 5–10 minutes, then sprinkle with the remaining parsley to serve.

BEEF KOFTA ROLLS

Kofta are delicious, either as kebabs in pitta or as meatballs in a spicy tomato sauce, but I thought I would try something a little different for a moreish snack. These sausage rolls are great for picnics or a weekend treat. I've used beef, but lamb mince also works well and the kofta mince recipe can be used for meatballs or kebabs for another meal. For a main course, serve with salad and Herby Tahini Sauce (see page 82), or for a punchy drizzle try my Hot Green Sauce (see page 136).

MAKES 8

2 tbsp plain flour,
    for dusting
1 x 320g ready-made
    puff pastry sheet
1 egg, beaten
vegetable oil, for greasing
2 tbsp sesame seeds

For the kofta mince
400g minced beef
½ red onion, grated
2 garlic cloves, grated
1 egg, beaten
1 thick slice of day-old
    white bread, crusts
    removed and made
    into breadcrumbs
    (either coarsely grated
    or briefly whizzed in
    a food processor)
1 tbsp finely chopped
    fresh flat-leaf parsley
1 tbsp finely chopped
    fresh mint
1 tsp pul biber/Aleppo
    pepper (or dried
    chilli flakes)
1 tsp ground cumin
1 tsp ground coriander
½ tsp sumac
zest of ½ lemon
¼ tsp bicarbonate of soda
sea salt and freshly
    ground black pepper

First, make the kofta mince. Combine all the kofta ingredients in a large mixing bowl, seasoning generously with salt and black pepper. Mix with your hands for a few minutes, ensuring that everything is well combined. If the mixture is too wet, add a few more breadcrumbs or a little flour.

On a lightly floured work surface, unroll the pastry sheet and cut in half lengthways into two long strips.

Divide the meat mixture in half. Arrange each half down the middle of each pastry strip in a long sausage shape. Roll each piece of pastry tightly around each meat sausage so that you finish with the joins underneath. Brush the edges with the beaten egg and press lightly to seal the seams. Cut each roll into four even lengths and transfer to a lightly oiled baking tray with the seam underneath. Chill for 20–25 minutes.

Meanwhile, preheat the oven to 200°C/180°C fan/gas 6.

Score each chilled sausage roll twice across the top, taking care not to cut all the way through. Brush with the remaining egg and sprinkle with the sesame seeds.

Bake for 30–35 minutes, or until the rolls are golden, crispy and cooked through (cover loosely with foil if you find they are browning too quickly near the end of cooking). Leave to rest for 5 minutes before serving.

ZA'ATAR SCHNITZEL WITH HOT GREEN SAUCE

Za'atar is an intense spice blend with thyme and sesame seeds, used frequently in the cuisine of Jordan and its surrounding countries. It adds an aromatic, tangy flavour to the crispy chicken coating in this dish. My herby hot sauce is a punchy accompaniment, inspired by a Middle-Eastern *zhoug* or *shatta*. The sauce recipe below makes plenty and leftovers can be used as an accompaniment for other recipes in this book (it can be kept in the fridge in an airtight container for up to two weeks), but feel free to halve the ingredients to make less. Serve with a mixed salad and fries.

SERVES 4

4 skinless and boneless
    chicken breasts
4 tbsp plain flour
3 tsp za'atar spice blend
    (or use a combination of
    sumac and dried thyme)
150g fine dried
    breadcrumbs
2 tsp sesame seeds
    (optional)
2 eggs, beaten
vegetable or sunflower oil,
    for frying
sea salt and freshly
    ground black pepper

For the Hot Green Sauce
3–4 large medium–hot
    green chillies
2 garlic cloves, peeled
100g fresh coriander,
    roughly chopped
100g fresh flat-leaf parsley,
    roughly chopped
½ tsp salt
½ tsp black pepper
seeds from 3–4 cardamom
    pods, crushed
½ tsp ground cumin
4–6 tbsp olive oil
juice of ½ lemon,
    or to taste

To serve
mixed salad
fries

First, make the Hot Green Sauce. Put the chillies, garlic, fresh herbs, salt, pepper and spices into a food processor and blitz to a coarse paste. Add 3–4 tablespoons of the olive oil and stir to combine. Add more olive oil if needed – you are looking for the consistency of a wet pesto. Squeeze in the lemon juice to taste. Set aside.

Place the chicken breasts on a board covered with baking parchment, flatten out the fillets and cover with another piece of parchment. Bash with a rolling pin or the bottom of a pan until they are about 5–6mm thick.

On a plate, mix the flour with 1 teaspoon of the za'atar and ½ teaspoon each of salt and pepper. On another plate, mix the breadcrumbs with the remaining 2 teaspoons of za'atar and the sesame seeds. Put the beaten eggs into a third shallow plate. Coat the chicken first in the seasoned flour, shaking off any excess. Dip the floured chicken into the eggs, making sure it is fully covered, then dip into the breadcrumb mixture and toss to completely coat. Place on a plate and chill in the fridge until ready to cook.

Fill a large deep frying pan with oil to a depth of 1.5cm and set over a medium–high heat. Once the oil is hot (but not smoking), fry the schnitzels (one or two at a time) for 3–4 minutes on each side until golden and the chicken is cooked through. Drain on kitchen paper and keep warm while you cook the remaining chicken.

Alternatively, place the schnitzels on a lightly oiled baking tray and bake in an oven heated to 220°C/200°C fan/gas 7 for 15–18 minutes, turning the schnitzels halfway through.

Serve the schnitzels with a mixed salad and fries with the Hot Green Sauce on the side.

TIP: To make a fiery 'red' version of the hot sauce, swap the green chillies for red and add ½ teaspoon of dried chilli flakes.

SPANISH-STYLE CHICKEN WITH SAFFRON POTATOES

Now, whenever I cook this dish it takes me right back to my outdoor kitchen at the Alhambra Palace Hotel, with its perfectly positioned terrace overlooking the stunning city of Grenada. The food of Andalucía is a reflection of its history and culture and there is a big influence from North Africa. This dish combines the spices of Moorish Cuisine – cinnamon and saffron – with Spanish olives, sherry and raisins to make a beautiful meal packed full of Mediterranean flavour. Perfect with the aromatic Saffron Potatoes.

SERVES 4

1 tbsp olive oil
1 onion, cut in half
    then thinly sliced
8 boneless chicken thighs,
    skin on
a good splash of dry sherry
3 tomatoes, diced
1 green chilli, thinly sliced
2 tbsp raisins
a large handful of green
    and black olives
1 cinnamon stick
1 tsp runny honey
a good pinch of saffron
1 tbsp sherry vinegar
150ml chicken stock
a handful fresh coriander,
    roughly chopped
2 tbsp flaked almonds,
    toasted
sea salt and freshly
    ground black pepper

For the Saffron Potatoes
a large pinch of saffron
300ml hot chicken or
    vegetable stock
2–3 tbsp olive oil
4 medium potatoes,
    peeled and cut into
    2.5-cm chunks
2 tbsp chopped fresh
    flat-leaf parsley
sea salt and freshly
    ground black pepper

First, cook the chicken. Heat the oil for the chicken in a large sautè pan or deep frying pan over a medium heat, add the onion and cook for 6–8 minutes until soft and golden. Remove from the pan and set aside.

Add the chicken, skin-side down, to the same pan and cook for about 6–8 minutes until golden. Turn the chicken over and cook for 2 minutes on the other side, then add the dry sherry and cook until the alcohol has evaporated. Return the onions to the pan and add the tomatoes, chilli, raisins, olives, cinnamon stick, honey, saffron, sherry vinegar and stock. Season with salt and pepper. Bring to the boil, then reduce the heat and simmer for 25–30 minutes until the chicken is tender, turning the chicken halfway through. Check the seasoning.

Meanwhile, make the potatoes. Add the saffron to the hot stock and leave to steep for 5 minutes, to allow the flavour to infuse.

Heat the oil for the potatoes in a sautè or deep frying pan over a medium heat, add the potatoes and cook on all sides until golden brown, about 6–8 minutes. Add the saffron-infused stock and a pinch of salt and bring to the boil, then simmer for 20 minutes until the liquid has evaporated and the potatoes are cooked through.

To serve, sprinkle the chicken with the coriander and flaked almonds. Season the potatoes with salt and pepper, stir through the chopped parsley and serve with the chicken.

SIRLOIN STEAK, CRUSHED POTATOES & RED PEPPER ROMESCO SAUCE

Romesco sauce is a classic Spanish sauce popular throughout the Mediterranean. Traditionally made from slow-roasted tomatoes, I'm using a jar of roasted red peppers for a quick and punchy accompaniment to the steak and crispy potatoes. Any leftover sauce can be stored in an airtight container in the fridge for a week. It's also great with chicken or fish, or try stirring through some cooked pasta for a tasty vegan meal.

SERVES 4

olive oil, for greasing
   and drizzling
700g baby new potatoes
1 tsp fresh thyme leaves
4 x 200g sirloin steaks
1 tbsp butter, or more
   if cooking in batches
   (optional)
sea salt and freshly
   ground black pepper
watercress, to serve

**For the Red Pepper
   Romesco Sauce**
35g blanched almonds
1 slice of bread, toasted
   and crusts removed
2–3 roasted red peppers
   from a jar (approx. 175g)
1 large garlic clove
½ tsp sweet/hot smoked
   paprika
½ red chilli, de-seeded
   and roughly chopped
1 tbsp chopped fresh
   flat-leaf parsley leaves
1 tbsp sherry vinegar
   or red wine vinegar
3–4 tbsp olive oil
½ lemon, for squeezing
sea salt and freshly
   ground black pepper

Preheat the oven to 220°C/200°C fan/gas 7 and lightly grease a baking tray with olive oil.

Put the potatoes into a large saucepan of water over a medium heat, bring to the boil and cook for 12–14 minutes until tender. Drain well, then tip the potatoes onto the prepared baking tray and use a potato masher or large fork to gently squash each potato until it flattens and splits slightly but remains in one piece. Drizzle with olive oil, sprinkle over the thyme and season with salt and pepper. Bake in the oven for 20–25 minutes, depending on the size of your potatoes, until crispy and golden.

Meanwhile, make the romesco sauce. In a dry pan over a medium heat, toast the almonds for about 2 minutes. Keep an eye on them so they don't burn. Put the toasted almonds, bread, peppers, garlic, paprika, chilli, parsley and vinegar in a blender and blitz until you have a paste. With the motor running, drizzle in enough of the olive oil to make a smooth, but still slightly textured, sauce. Season with salt and pepper and add lemon juice to taste. Set aside.

Heat a griddle pan or large frying pan over a high heat until just beginning to smoke. Drizzle the steaks with olive oil and season generously with salt and pepper. Add to the pan, turn the heat down to medium–high and cook for 1 minute. Turn the steak and cook for 1 minute, then add the butter to the pan (if using) and cook for a further 2 minutes on each side for medium, basting constantly with the pan juices, or until cooked to your liking. If cooking in batches, you may need to add more butter to the pan as needed. Once cooked, remove from the pan, season with pepper and leave to rest for 3–4 minutes before serving with the potatoes, a handful of watercress and the romesco sauce.

CHICKEN SHAWARMA WRAPS
WITH TAHINI YOGHURT DIP

Chicken Shawarma is a popular spiced kebab found all over the Middle-Eastern Mediterranean. It's easy to make and you can mix up the spices to suit your taste. It's also great with beef or lamb if you fancy a change. You can serve the shawarma with rice and salad or these wraps make a great lunch or a Friday-night dinner – no more trips to the kebab shop!

SERVES 4

4 skinless and boneless
   chicken thighs
2 skinless and boneless
   chicken breasts
olive oil, for greasing
   and frying
sea salt and freshly
   ground black pepper

For the marinade
½ tsp ground cardamom
2 tsp ground cumin
2 tsp ground coriander
½ tsp ground cinnamon
1 tsp cayenne pepper
1 tsp ground turmeric
zest and juice of ½ lemon
2 garlic cloves, grated
3 tbsp olive oil

**For the Tahini
   Yoghurt Dip**
150g Greek yoghurt
2 tbsp tahini
1 garlic clove (smoked
   if you have it), grated
1 tbsp chopped fresh
   flat-leaf parsley
juice of ½ lemon

To serve
4 large flatbread wraps
a handful of shredded
   crisp lettuce
½ small red cabbage,
   shredded
2 tomatoes, sliced
½ red onion, thinly sliced
1 tbsp roughly chopped
   coriander leaves

In a large bowl, mix together all the ingredients for the chicken marinade and add the chicken. Season with salt and pepper and mix well, ensuring that the chicken is well coated. Cover and leave to marinate in the fridge for 2 hours, if you have the time.

Meanwhile, make the tahini yoghurt dip. Put all of the ingredients in a bowl and mix until well combined. Add a little water to loosen if needed. Chill until ready to serve.

Preheat the oven to 200°C/180°C fan/gas 6 and lightly oil a roasting tray.

Put the marinated chicken onto the prepared roasting tray and bake for 10–12 minutes. Remove from the oven and let rest for a few minutes, then cut the chicken into thin slices.

Heat a little oil in a frying pan over a medium–high heat and add the chicken slices and any cooking juices. Fry for 3–4 minutes until slightly crispy and golden brown.

To serve, warm the flatbread wraps and fill with slices of chicken, lettuce, cabbage, tomato, onion and coriander and a good dollop of tahini yoghurt dip. Add some Hot Green Sauce (see page 136) too, if you like.

HARISSA LEMON CHICKEN SKEWERS WITH GLAZED AUBERGINES & GARLIC-MINT SAUCE

While in Morocco, I just had to cook a dish using harissa –the delicious North-African spice paste made from chillies and fragrant spices. The vibrant tang of preserved lemons works beautifully in a spicy marinade and these chicken skewers and fire-glazed cumin and honey aubergines certainly went down a treat with the crew. This harissa marinade is also great with lamb or vegetables.

SERVES 4

For the Harissa Lemon Chicken Skewers
2 tbsp Greek yoghurt
1 tsp ground cumin
1 tsp hot smoked paprika
1 garlic clove, grated
1 heaped tbsp Moroccan harissa paste
1 preserved lemon, chopped
2 tbsp olive oil
4 skinless chicken breasts, cut into 2.5-cm cubes
sea salt and freshly ground black pepper

For the Glazed Aubergines
4 baby aubergines, quartered
2 tsp ground cumin
2 tsp runny honey
a good pinch each of salt and pepper
1 tbsp olive oil

For the Garlic-Mint Sauce
6 tbsp Greek yogurt
2 garlic cloves, grated
2 tbsp chopped fresh mint leaves
juice of ½ lemon
sea salt, to taste
a sprinkle of sweet/hot smoked paprika, to serve

To serve
pitta breads
a few mint sprigs
lemon wedges

Preheat a barbecue or a griddle pan over a medium–high heat. If not using the barbecue, additionally preheat the oven to 200°C/180°C fan/gas 6.

First, marinate the chicken for the skewers. In a large bowl, mix together the yoghurt, cumin, smoked paprika, garlic, harissa paste, preserved lemon, olive oil and a pinch each of salt and pepper, stirring to combine. Toss the chicken cubes in the marinade until coated, then cover and leave to marinate for at least 20 minutes.

For the aubergines, place the aubergine wedges in a separate bowl, add the cumin and honey and mix together until coated. Season with a good pinch each of salt and pepper and drizzle with the oil and mix again.

Next, make the garlic mint sauce. In a small bowl, whisk together all of the ingredients except the salt until well combined. Season with salt to taste and set aside.

Thread the chicken onto four skewers and place onto the hot barbecue or griddle pan. Cook for 5–6 minutes, then turn and cook the other side for a further 4–6 minutes until the chicken is cooked through.

Meanwhile, place the aubergines onto the barbecue and cook for 8–10 minutes, turning regularly, until golden and soft. If not using a barbecue, pop the aubergines onto a baking tray and into the oven for 15–20 minutes.

Serve the chicken skewers and glazed aubergines with the garlic mint sauce on the side, sprinkled with a little smoked paprika, with pitta breads, a few sprigs of mint and some lemon wedges for squeezing over.

ONE-POT ROSE HARISSA CHICKEN & APRICOT PILAF

With the flavours of a Moroccan tagine, this quick and easy one-pot is perfect for a mid-week supper. I'm using a ready-made harissa paste to add a depth of flavour and a smoky chilli kick. Rose harissa gives a special sweetness and aroma, but you can use ordinary harissa if you prefer and you can add more or less depending on how spicy you like it.

SERVES 4

50g pistachios or
  flaked almonds
2 tbsp olive oil
1 red onion, cut into
  8 wedges
1 tsp ground turmeric
8 skinless and boneless
  chicken thighs
1–2 tbsp rose harissa paste
350g basmati rice
80g soft dried apricots,
  halved
700ml chicken stock,
  plus extra as needed
1 cinnamon stick,
  broken in half
2 tbsp chopped fresh
  coriander leaves
sea salt and freshly
  ground black pepper

Preheat the oven to 200°C/180°C fan/gas 6.

In a large casserole over a medium heat, toast the pistachios or almonds for 1–2 minutes. Keep an eye on them to make sure they don't burn. Remove to a bowl and set aside.

Heat the oil in the casserole over a medium heat, add the red onion and cook for 4–6 minutes until softened but not coloured. Add the turmeric and cook for 30 seconds until fragrant, then add the chicken and cook for 4–6 minutes, turning until browned all over. Stir through the harissa paste, then add the rice, apricots and stock. Add the cinnamon stick, season with salt and a generous grinding of black pepper and stir. Bring to the boil, then remove from the heat, cover with a lid and bake in the oven for 20–25 minutes or until the chicken is cooked through and the rice is tender. Check halfway through the cooking time and add a little more stock if needed.

Remove the cinnamon stick, stir in the toasted pistachios or almonds, chopped coriander and check the seasoning. Serve garnished with coriander sprigs.

PORK CHOPS WITH THYME-ROASTED TOMATOES, BORLOTTI BEANS & KALE

Pork and beans – a classic combination. Here I've taken delicious and classic flavours from around the Med and combined them to make a tasty and satisfying dish. You can skip the roasting of the tomatoes if you're short on time, but it really does add a wonderful depth of flavour and sweetness.

SERVES 4

1 x 270g pack cherry vine tomatoes or baby plum tomatoes
4 tbsp olive oil
a pinch of dried chilli flakes
1 tsp fresh thyme leaves
4 garlic cloves: 2 thinly sliced; 2 peeled and smashed
200g young kale, stems removed and leaves shredded
1 x 400g tin borlotti beans, drained
175ml chicken or vegetable stock, or extra as needed
1 tbsp chopped fresh flat-leaf parsley, plus extra to serve
2 tsp sherry vinegar
4 bone-in pork chops, 2.5cm thick (at room temperature)
2 tbsp unsalted butter
sea salt and freshly ground black pepper

Preheat the oven to 220°C/200°C fan/gas 7.

Place the tomatoes in a roasting tray and drizzle with 1 tablespoon of the olive oil. Season with salt and a generous grinding of pepper, then sprinkle over the dried chilli flakes and half of the thyme and gently toss to combine. Roast for 15–18 minutes until blistered and soft. Remove from the oven and set aside.

Heat 2 tablespoons of the olive oil in a sauté pan or deep frying pan over a medium heat, add the sliced garlic and cook for 30 seconds until fragrant. Add the kale and cook for 3–4 minutes until the leaves start to wilt, then add the beans, the remaining thyme and add the stock. Simmer for 8–10 minutes (adding a little more stock if the pan starts to look dry). Stir in the parsley, vinegar and roasted tomatoes along with any of their pan juices and simmer for a further 2 minutes. Season with salt and pepper, then turn off the heat but leave on the hob to keep warm.

Meanwhile, generously season both sides of the pork chops with salt and pepper. Heat the remaining 1 tablespoon of olive oil in a large heavy-based frying pan or griddle pan over a high heat until hot. Add the pork, then reduce the heat to medium and cook for 1 minute before turning and searing the other side for 1 minute. Add the butter and the whole smashed garlic cloves to the pan and cook for a further 8–10 minutes, or until the pork is cooked through, turning and basting often in the juices. Remove the pork from the pan and allow to rest for 4–5 minutes.

To serve, spoon the beans, tomatoes and kale onto warmed plates, place the chops on top, drizzle with any pan juices and sprinkle with some extra parsley.

ROASTED PORCHETTA WITH POTATO, FENNEL & GREEN BEAN SALAD

While in Sardinia, chef Tiziano Vacca cooked us roasted suckling pig (*porceddu*) over a fire pit on the beach. Traditionally, the meat is first flavoured with myrtle, fennel and garlic before being roasted over an open fire with dried herb twigs and wood chips. It's a delicious dish but obviously not one that can be easily cooked at home. I've taken the flavours of the *porceddu* and used a shoulder of pork to create a wonderful roast – perfect for a family gathering. Porchetta is rich and is best served with bread and a light side dish. My roasted potato, fennel and green bean salad works perfectly.

SERVES 6–8

2 tsp fennel seeds
1 tsp black peppercorns
1 tbsp chopped fresh
    rosemary
3 tbsp chopped fresh
    flat-leaf parsley
2 tsp chopped fresh
    thyme leaves
4 garlic cloves, grated
40g salted butter
zest of 1 lemon
2.75kg boneless pork
    shoulder, rind scored
    (at room temperature)
sea salt

**For the Potato, Fennel
    and Green Bean Salad**
450g fine green beans,
    trimmed
1 fennel bulb, trimmed,
    cored and thinly sliced
650g fingerling, Anya,
    or Yukon Gold potatoes,
    washed and halved
    lengthways
1 garlic clove, thinly sliced
1 tsp fresh thyme leaves
2–3 tbsp olive oil
2 tbsp slivered or
    sliced almonds
juice of ½ lemon,
    or to taste
sea salt and freshly
    ground black pepper

Preheat the oven to 190°C/170°C fan/gas 5.

Grind the fennel seeds and peppercorns in a pestle and mortar until crushed. Transfer to a bowl and combine with the rosemary, parsley, thyme, garlic, butter, lemon zest and ½ teaspoon of salt.

Open out the pork shoulder on a board, rind-side down, and use a sharp knife to cut a few 2.5cm-deep incisions into the meat, but don't cut all the way through. Spread the herb mixture evenly over the interior of the pork, firmly pressing the paste into the cuts. Tightly roll the pork back up to enclose the filling and tie with kitchen string at 2cm intervals, working from both ends towards the centre; this keeps the meat in shape. Wipe off any excess moisture with kitchen paper and sprinkle with salt.

Place the pork in a roasting tin and roast for 2 hours 20 minutes in total (or 20 minutes per 450g plus an extra 20 minutes). For the last 20 minutes of cooking time, increase the oven temperature to 220°C/200°C fan/gas 7 until the pork is cooked through and tender with crispy crackling. Remove the pork from the oven, cover with foil and leave to rest in a warm place for 25–30 minutes. Reduce the oven temperature to 200°C/180°C/gas 6.

Meanwhile, make the salad. Blanche the green beans in a saucepan of salted boiling water for 3–4 minutes. Refresh under cold water and drain. Arrange the fennel and potatoes in a single layer in a large baking tray. Scatter over the garlic and thyme, drizzle with the olive oil and toss to evenly coat. Season with salt and pepper. Roast for 20 minutes, then add the nuts and green beans to the tray, toss together and roast for a further 5 minutes until the potatoes are lightly golden and tender. Squeeze over the lemon juice to taste and check the seasoning.

Carve the pork into slices and arrange on warmed plates, then spoon over the pan juices. Serve the roasted salad alongside.

CHARGRILLED LAMB STEAKS & ARTICHOKES WITH ROSEMARY & HONEY GLAZE

I just had to cook lamb while in Sardinia. The mountainous island is known for its sheepherding and the quality of the tender meat is fantastic. This recipe uses just a simple glaze to enhance the wonderful flavour. Lamb with artichokes is a much-loved combination on the island and a familiar sight on restaurant menus. The delicate sweet nutty taste of the artichoke complements the meat perfectly. Make sure you use a good-quality jar of chargrilled artichokes in oil.

SERVES 4

2 garlic cloves, grated
2 tsp chopped rosemary
    leaves, plus extra leaves
    to garnish
3 tbsp balsamic vinegar
4 tbsp extra-virgin olive oil
1 lemon: zest and juice
    of ½; plus ½ reserved
    for squeezing
4 lamb leg steaks
1 tbsp honey (thyme honey
    if you can get it)
6–8 artichoke hearts from a
    jar, drained and halved
a drizzle of olive oil,
    for frying
400g cabbage, such as
    Savoy or cavolo nero,
    finely shredded
sea salt and freshly
    ground black pepper

Put the garlic, rosemary, balsamic vinegar, extra-virgin olive oil, lemon zest and juice into a shallow dish or baking tray. Season with salt and pepper and add the lamb steaks. Toss to coat in the marinade, then cover and let marinate in the fridge for at least 2 hours or ideally overnight.

When ready to cook, heat a griddle pan over a medium–high heat until hot. Add the lamb and cook for 4 minutes on each side. Meanwhile, stir the honey into the leftover marinade and spoon a little over each lamb steak as it cooks. When the lamb is almost cooked, add the artichoke hearts to the pan and drizzle with a little of the marinade. Leave to char for 1 minute, then turn and cook the other side.

Remove the lamb and set aside to rest for 4–5 minutes.

Heat a drizzle of olive oil in a frying pan over a medium heat, then add the cabbage and a squeeze of juice from the reserved lemon half. Season with salt and pepper and allow to wilt until just tender.

To serve, place the cabbage in the centre of each plate, sit a lamb steak on top and spoon the artichokes and any pan juices around the sides. Scatter over a few rosemary leaves to finish.

CHARGRILLED SUMAC LAMB CUTLETS WITH TABBOULEH

Tabbouleh is traditionally a Levantine dish that's become popular all over the Mediterranean. In Jordan and around the Middle East it's served as part of a mezze, but I'm serving it as a herby, fresh-tasting salad to complement the zesty lamb. The herbs are the star of this salad. Sumac grows wild in Jordan and provides a tangy lemon flavour to meat, fish, vegetables or dips. This dish is also great for a barbecue – just cook the chops on the hot grill for 3–4 minutes on each side or until cooked to your liking.

SERVES 4

3 tbsp olive oil
2 tsp sumac
a good pinch of dried
    chilli flakes
zest of 1 lemon
8–12 lamb cutlets
    (depending on size)
sea salt and freshly
    ground black pepper

For the Tabbouleh
100g bulgur wheat, cooked
    according to the packet
    instructions
3 tomatoes, chopped
1 small red onion,
    finely diced
a large bunch of fresh
    flat-leaf parsley, chopped
a small bunch of fresh
    mint, chopped
juice of 1 lemon
a drizzle of honey
3 tbsp extra-virgin olive oil
1 red chilli, finely chopped
sea salt and freshly
    ground black pepper

For the dressing
4 tbsp natural yoghurt
1 small garlic clove, grated
juice of ½ lemon
a pinch of sumac
1 tbsp mint leaves,
    finely chopped
sea salt and freshly
    ground black pepper

To serve
1 red chilli, finely sliced
lemon wedges

In a large bowl, mix together the olive oil, sumac, chilli flakes and lemon zest and season with salt and pepper. Add the lamb cutlets and toss to make sure they are well coated. Set aside to marinate for at least 20 minutes.

Meanwhile, make the tabbouleh. Place all of the ingredients except the seasoning into a bowl and stir to combine. Season to taste.

Heat a griddle pan over a medium–high heat. Cook the lamb for 4–5 minutes on each side. Once cooked, set the lamb aside to rest for a couple of minutes.

To make the dressing, put the yoghurt in a small bowl with the garlic, lemon juice and sumac and whisk in enough water to make a smooth dressing. Stir through the mint, season to taste and set aside.

Serve the lamb chops on top of the tabbouleh with a good drizzle of the dressing. Scatter over sliced chilli and serve lemon wedges on the side.

SARDINIAN PASTA SHELLS WITH SAUSAGE, TOMATO & FENNEL SAUCE

I had the pleasure of making fresh Sardinian *chiusoni* pasta with the wonderful Erica and Alessandro from Agriturismo Stazzu Li Paladini in Olbia. Usually called *malloreddus* or *gnocchetti sardi*, they are small conch-shaped pasta shells that are ridged on one side so they can hold onto lots of sauce. If you can't find any, then a small pasta like *orecchiette* or *cavatelli* works well. This is a typical Sardinian dish made with sausage, fennel and plenty of pecorino.

SERVES 4

2 tbsp olive oil
1 onion, chopped
2 garlic cloves,
    grated or minced
1 tbsp fennel seeds
1 tsp finely chopped
    rosemary leaves
400g good-quality
    sausages, skinned
    and roughly chopped
a splash of white wine
1 x 400g tin chopped
    tomatoes
400g chiusoni, malloreddus
    or gnocchetti sardi pasta
    (or similar short pasta)
a pinch of black pepper

To serve
pecorino cheese, grated
fennel fronds

Heat the oil in a sauté pan or deep frying pan over a medium heat, add the onion and cook for 4–6 minutes until softened but not coloured. Stir in the garlic, fennel seeds and rosemary and cook until fragrant, then remove from the pan to a bowl and set aside.

Add the sausagemeat to the pan and fry until it begins to brown, using a wooden spoon to stir and break down the meat. Cook for 3–4 minutes until it begins to go a little crispy round the edges, then return the onion mixture to the pan. Add a splash of white wine and allow to bubble, then stir in the tomatoes and simmer for 10 minutes.

Meanwhile, cook the pasta according to the packet instructions until al dente.

Once cooked, add the pasta to the sauce and gently stir to coat. Season with a little pepper and serve in warmed pasta bowls, topped with grated pecorino and a few fennel fronds.

ONE-PAN BAKED CHICKEN ORZO WITH CHORIZO & OLIVES

Orzo is popular throughout the Mediterranean and, although shaped like a large grain of rice, it's actually a short form of pasta. Despite being Italian in nature, this comforting dish is packed with the flavours of Spain and is an easy meal to make for any day of the week. It's a tasty combination of smoky chicken, velvety pasta and salty olives and cheese. What's more, it's all cooked in one pan. Sounds good to me! Feel free to add some red chilli or dried chilli flakes, if you like things spicy.

SERVES 4

4–6 skinless and boneless chicken thighs (depending on size)
2 tbsp olive oil, plus extra for drizzling
1½ tsp sweet smoked paprika
2 tsp dried oregano
1 onion, chopped
100g spicy cooking chorizo, skinned and sliced
1 red pepper, de-seeded and chopped
2 garlic cloves, finely chopped
1 tsp tomato purée
1 x 400g tin cherry tomatoes
500ml hot chicken stock, or more as needed
250g orzo pasta
8–10 Spanish green olives, pitted and halved
4 tbsp chopped fresh flat-leaf parsley
60g Manchego cheese (or Parmesan), grated
sea salt and freshly ground black pepper

Preheat the oven to 200°C/180°C fan/gas 6.

Place the chicken thighs in a large bowl with a drizzle of olive oil and 1 teaspoon each of the paprika and oregano. Season with salt and pepper and mix well to coat the chicken. Set aside.

Heat 1 tablespoon of the oil in a large casserole dish over a medium–high heat, add the chicken thighs and cook for 3–4 minutes on each side until lightly browned. Remove from the pan and set aside.

Reduce the heat to medium and add the remaining olive oil to the pan, then add the onion and cook for 4–6 minutes until softened but not coloured. Add the chorizo and cook for 1 minute, then add the pepper, garlic and remaining paprika and cook for 2–3 minutes. Stir through the tomato purée, remaining oregano, tinned tomatoes and stock, then season with salt and pepper. Bring to the boil, then add the orzo, giving everything a good stir.

Nestle the chicken thighs on top of the orzo mixture and put the casserole in the oven to bake, uncovered, for 25–30 minutes or until the chicken is cooked through and the pasta is cooked al dente. Check halfway through cooking and add a little more stock if needed.

Remove from the oven and allow to sit for a few minutes before stirring in the olives and half the chopped parsley. Scatter with grated cheese and remaining parsley then serve at the table for everyone to share.

CAPRESE BEEF BURGERS WITH PESTO MAYO

Sometimes we all need a treat and a good home-made burger is perfect for a Friday night in with friends or family. These Italian-style burgers are inspired by the wonderful ingredients in an Italian Caprese salad – fresh tomatoes, basil and creamy mozzarella. You can dial up the heat by adding some chilli flakes to the burger, if you like. To prevent your burgers puffing up during cooking, make a thumb print indentation in the centre of each one – this will ensure you get a nice even patty.

SERVES 4

4 heaped tbsp mayonnaise
1 heaped tbsp good-quality basil pesto
zest of ½ lemon
750g good-quality (20%-fat) minced beef
1 small onion, finely chopped
1 tbsp chopped fresh flat-leaf parsley
1 tbsp olive oil, plus extra for brushing
sea salt and freshly ground black pepper

To serve
4 ciabatta buns, lightly toasted
a handful of rocket leaves
1 x 125g mozzarella ball, thinly sliced
1 avocado, stone removed, thinly sliced (optional)
2 vine tomatoes, sliced

In a small bowl, mix the mayonnaise with the pesto and lemon zest. Cover and chill until ready to serve.

Combine the beef, onion and parsley in a bowl and season well. Use your hands to mix until the meat starts to hold together well. Divide the mixture into four and shape each piece into a 10-cm flat disc, either by hand or by pressing the mixture into a metal pastry cutter. Brush each burger with oil, put onto a plate, then cover and chill for at least 20 minutes.

When ready to cook, heat the oil in a frying pan or griddle pan over a medium–high heat, then place the burgers in the pan and reduce the heat to medium. Use a spatula to press down on the burgers lightly and cook for 3–4 minutes on each side for a medium burger.

To serve, spread a little of the pesto mayonnaise on the bottom half of each ciabatta bun. Top with the burgers and then the slices of mozzarella and a few rocket leaves. Finish with slices of tomato and avocado and a good dollop of the pesto mayonnaise before putting on the top half of the bun. Enjoy with a side salad or fries.

MOROCCAN LEMON CHICKEN, CARROT & BABY POTATO TRAYBAKE

The warm spices of the Marrakesh souks are brought together in this easy and satisfying traybake and the preserved lemon adds a lovely freshness. Preserved lemons are available in jars from the supermarket, but if you don't have any you can use a fresh lemon, cut into wedges. Mix a teaspoon of harissa paste through some Greek yoghurt for a tasty drizzle and serve with your favourite couscous. (There's a fantastic brand of instant couscous available in the supermarkets!)

SERVES 4–6

700g baby or new potatoes, scrubbed and halved
500g baby heritage, rainbow or chantenay carrots, scrubbed
4 garlic cloves, sliced
1 large preserved lemon, rind only, finely chopped
1 large red onion, cut into 8 wedges
olive oil, for drizzling
1 tbsp ras el hanout
½ tsp coriander seeds, crushed
6 skin-on, bone-in chicken thighs or fat drumsticks (also see Tip)
100ml hot chicken stock
6–8 dates (preferably Medjool), pitted and halved
sea salt and freshly ground black pepper

To serve
couscous
2 tbsp fresh coriander leaves, roughly chopped
harissa yoghurt (see note in introduction)

Preheat the oven to 200°C/180°C fan/gas 6.

Place the potatoes, carrots, garlic, lemon and onion into a large baking tray or dish. Drizzle with olive oil, sprinkle over half of the ras el hanout and all of the coriander seeds, season with salt and pepper and toss to coat.

Put the chicken pieces into a separate bowl and drizzle with a little oil, then sprinkle over the remaining ras el hanout and rub it into the skin. Season with salt and pepper.

Arrange the chicken pieces between the vegetables, skin-side up, and drizzle with a little more oil. Pour the chicken stock around the chicken and place the tray in the oven.

Bake for 30 minutes, then remove the tray from the oven, toss the vegetables and scatter over the dates. Add a splash more stock if needed. Return to the oven and bake for a further 15–20 minutes or until the chicken is golden and cooked through, depending on the size of your chicken thighs (the juices should run clear when pierced).

Serve hot with couscous and any pan juices poured over the top. Scatter with the coriander and drizzle with harissa yoghurt.

TIP: You can use chicken breasts, if you prefer – just roast the veg for 30 minutes before adding the breasts to the tin and cooking for 15–20 minutes or until cooked through.

MOLASSES-GLAZED STEAK, FIG & WALNUT SALAD WITH BLUE CHEESE

This is a combination of Italian and Middle-Eastern flavours and I think it really works – the pomegranate molasses and balsamic creating a tart yet sweet glaze for the steak, figs and walnuts. It makes a wonderful sharing dish for a dinner party. You can swap the figs for vacuum-packed figs if you can't find fresh. The marinated steak is fantastic cooked on the barbecue.

SERVES 4

3 tbsp extra-virgin olive oil, plus extra for drizzling
1 tsp fresh thyme leaves, chopped
1 garlic clove, grated
½ tsp sumac, plus extra to serve
3 tbsp balsamic vinegar
3 tbsp pomegranate molasses
2 tsp runny honey
700g beef steak (approx. 3 sirloin steaks)
4 ripe figs, quartered
60g toasted walnuts, roughly chopped
a pinch of dried chilli flakes
a large handful of rocket leaves
a large handful of baby spinach leaves
80g Gorgonzola or similar blue cheese
seeds from ½ pomegranate
sea salt and freshly ground black pepper

In a bowl, mix together the extra-virgin olive oil, thyme, garlic, sumac, 2 tablespoons of the balsamic vinegar, 2 tablespoons of the pomegranate molasses and 1 teaspoon of the honey. Add the steaks, season with salt and pepper and mix well to coat. Cover and place in the fridge to marinate for at least 30 minutes, preferably longer, if you have the time.

Heat a large frying pan over a medium–high heat until hot. Shaking off any excess marinade from the steaks, add them to the pan and cook for 2–3 minutes on each side (depending on how you like your steak cooked). Remove the steaks from the pan, cover loosely with foil to keep warm and let rest for 4–5 minutes. Once rested, cut into 1-cm slices.

To the same pan, add the figs, walnuts and chilli flakes and stir in the remaining balsamic vinegar, pomegranate molasses and honey along with 75ml water. Stir to deglaze the pan and bring to a simmer, then cook over a medium heat for 2–3 minutes to reduce the sauce. Remove from the heat.

Scatter the salad leaves over a serving platter and arrange the steak slices on top. Spoon over the warm figs, walnuts and their sauce, then scatter over the crumbled blue cheese and pomegranate seeds and drizzle over a little more extra-virgin olive oil, if desired. Season with salt and a pinch of sumac and serve immediately.

MOORISH BARBECUED LAMB KEBABS WITH DUKKAH TOMATO SALAD

The Moors brought many spices, herbs and cooking techniques over to Andalucía, most of which are still popular in today's cuisine. These tasty kebabs are inspired by the flavours of Spanish *pinchitos* or *pinchos morunos* – a tapas-style spiced meat skewer found on many a snack-bar menu. I've made them into larger kebabs for a satisfying main course and they're perfect for a barbecue or can be cooked on a griddle pan if the weather isn't ideal. The North-African spice dukkah brings a nice crunch to the simple tomato and onion accompaniment. The kebabs are also delicious made with pork or chicken.

**SERVES 4
(MAKES 8 SKEWERS)**

1 tbsp sherry vinegar
(or lemon juice)
3 tbsp extra-virgin olive oil,
plus extra for drizzling
2 garlic cloves, grated
2 tsp chopped fresh oregano
(or 1 tsp dried)
2 tsp cumin seeds, crushed
2 tsp sweet smoked paprika
1 tsp cayenne or hot smoked
paprika, plus an extra
pinch for the yoghurt
dressing
1 tsp ground turmeric
800g lamb, trimmed of
excess fat, cut into
3-cm cubes
4 large vine tomatoes,
sliced
½ red onion, thinly sliced
zest and juice of ½ lemon
1–2 tbsp of Dukkah (shop-
bought or see page 119)
1 tbsp of chopped fresh
coriander
4 tbsp natural yoghurt
sea salt and freshly
ground black pepper

In a large bowl mix together the vinegar, oil, garlic, oregano, cumin seeds, paprika, cayenne pepper and turmeric, and season generously with black pepper and salt. Add the lamb and toss to coat. Cover and marinate in the fridge for at least 1 hour, but preferably longer if you have the time.

Preheat the barbecue (or a griddle pan to medium–hot).

Thread the marinated lamb cubes onto eight skewers. Place on the barbecue grill (or griddle pan) and cook for 8–10 minutes or until cooked to your liking, turning occasionally.

Meanwhile, arrange the tomato and onion slices on a serving platter, sprinkle with a little salt and lemon zest and drizzle with extra-virgin olive oil. Scatter with the dukkah and coriander and squeeze over a little of the lemon juice to taste.

Put the yoghurt into a small bowl and stir in another squeeze of lemon juice and a pinch of cayenne pepper to taste, then season with salt and pepper.

Serve the kebabs with the tomato salad, drizzled with the yoghurt dressing.

SAUSAGE, CHESTNUT & HARICOT BEAN CASSOULET

When visiting Corsica, I tried a deliciously rich sausage stew. The local *figatellu* sausage is a chestnut-smoked, pork liver sausage that's difficult to find elsewhere, so I've recreated the flavour by adding chestnuts, bacon and a touch of smoky paprika to a simplified and quick cassoulet. Do try and get good-quality pork sausages because it really does make a difference. This is great comfort food – serve with a nice glass of red wine and enjoy.

SERVES 4–6

2 tbsp olive oil, plus extra for drizzling
8 good-quality thick pork sausages
150g thick-cut streaky bacon, chopped, or bacon lardons
150g cooked whole chestnuts, quartered
1 large onion, diced
2 carrots, diced
1 tsp hot smoked paprika
1 tsp herbes de Provence (or dried thyme)
3 garlic cloves, grated
400ml hot chicken or vegetable stock
1 tbsp tomato purée
1 x 400g tin chopped tomatoes
1 tsp light brown sugar
1 tbsp Dijon mustard
2 tbsp chopped fresh flat-leaf parsley
2 x 400g tins haricot, butter or cannellini beans, drained and rinsed
100g bread with crusts, broken into chunks
sea salt and freshly ground black pepper

Preheat the oven to 200°C/180°C fan/gas 6.

Heat 1 tablespoon of the oil in a large, deep non-stick frying pan or sauté pan over a medium heat, add the sausages and fry until browned all over. Remove from the pan and place in a 2-litre casserole dish or lasagne dish. Fry the bacon and chestnuts in the same pan for 3–4 minutes, then transfer to the casserole dish.

Add a further 1 tablespoon of oil to the pan, add the onions and carrots and cook for 4–6 minutes until softened but not coloured. Stir in ½ teaspoon of the paprika, the herbes de Provence and garlic and cook for 30 seconds until fragrant. Add the stock, tomato purée, tinned tomatoes, sugar, mustard and 1 tablespoon of the parsley, and stir well, scraping up any flavours from the bottom of the pan. Bring to the boil, then add the beans, season with salt and pepper, and simmer for 8–10 minutes.

Transfer the sauce to the casserole and stir to combine all the ingredients.

Put the bread into a processor and blitz a few times until you have coarse breadcrumbs. Mix the breadcrumbs with the remaining 1 tablespoon of parsley, ½ teaspoon of paprika, a drizzle of olive oil and a small pinch of salt and pepper, then sprinkle over the casserole in an even layer.

Bake for 20–25 minutes until the top is bubbling and golden. Serve immediately.

MIDDLE-EASTERN SLOW-ROASTED LAMB

I had an amazing time visiting the Bedouin in Jordan and learning how they make their *zarb* – a traditional way of slow-cooking meat in an underground pit. The lamb was so succulent. I've recreated the flavours with a slow-cooked roast lamb that is tender and delicious. Try serving with my Quick Flatbreads and Roasted Tomato Salsa (see page 34), Hummus (see page 33) and/or couscous.

SERVES 4-6

1 bone-in leg or shoulder
    of lamb, approx. 2kg
2 red onions, each cut
    into 1-cm slices
1 garlic bulb, halved
    widthways
3 thyme sprigs
1 lemon, cut into
    1-cm slices
500ml lamb stock,
    or more as needed
sea salt and freshly
    ground black pepper

For the marinade
2 garlic cloves, grated
3 tbsp olive oil, plus
    extra for drizzling
zest and juice of 1 lemon
2 tbsp za'atar
1 tsp ground cumin
1 tsp ground cinnamon
2 tbsp pomegranate
    molasses
sea salt and freshly
    ground black pepper

To serve
2 tbsp roughly chopped
    fresh coriander
pickled chillies
seeds from 1 pomegranate
Greek yoghurt

First, make the marinade. In a bowl, combine the grated garlic, olive oil, lemon zest and juice, za'atar, cumin, cinnamon, pomegranate molasses and a good pinch of salt and pepper.

Place the lamb in a large bowl and pierce the flesh in several places with a sharp knife. Pour over the marinade and rub lightly into the flesh. Cover and marinate in the fridge for at least 2 hours.

Preheat the oven to 170°C/150°C fan/gas 4.

Put the onion, garlic bulb halves, thyme sprigs and lemon slices in the bottom of a large roasting tray. Sit the marinated lamb on top, season the meat with salt and pepper, then drizzle with olive oil. Pour the stock around the lamb, cover with parchment, then seal with a layer of foil. Roast in the oven for 4½ hours, checking two or three times during that time to baste with the pan juices and adding more stock if needed.

Remove from the oven and check that the lamb is tender (it should start to come apart when pried with a fork). If tender, remove the foil and parchment and baste again, then increase the oven temperature to 200°C/180°C fan/gas 6. Return the lamb to the oven and roast, uncovered, for 30 minutes or until browned.

Remove the lamb from the oven, cover and leave to rest for 20 minutes.

Slice or shred the rested lamb, then arrange on a sharing platter, scattered with coriander, pickled chillies and pomegranate seeds. If you wish, mix the onions in the tray with the juices and serve with the lamb. Drizzle with Greek yoghurt just before serving.

DESSERTS
& DRINKS

ALMOND & CHOCOLATE CANISTRELLI BISCUITS

These crunchy little biscuits are a speciality of Corsica and the recipe can be changed to include orange, hazelnuts, herbs or aniseed. They're very similar to Italian biscotti but slightly softer and have an earthy flavour from the wholemeal and chestnut flour. The recipe doesn't contain any eggs or butter, so they are great for a vegan treat and perfect biscuits for dunking!

MAKES 30–35 BISCUITS

300g plain wholemeal flour, plus extra for dusting
100g chestnut or almond flour
2 tsp baking powder
170g light brown sugar
1 tsp salt
zest of 1 lemon
140ml olive oil
110ml vegan dry white wine
60g almonds, roughly chopped
50g vegan chocolate chips

Preheat the oven to 180°C/160°C fan/gas 4 and line a baking tray with baking parchment.

In a large bowl, combine the flours, baking powder, sugar, salt and lemon zest. Form a well in the centre and pour in the olive oil and wine. Stir the liquids into the dry ingredients, then add the chopped almonds and chocolate chips. Work gently with a spoon until the dough comes together, then use your hands to bring everything together into a ball. You may need to add a splash of water if the dough is a little dry.

Tip the dough onto a lightly floured work surface, then flatten or gently roll the dough to 2cm thick. Slice the dough into 2.5-cm strips and then cut into square or diamond shapes. Transfer to the prepared baking tray leaving a gap in between.

Bake for 15 minutes, then reduce the heat to 160°C/140°C fan/gas 3 and bake for a further 15–18 minutes until golden brown.

Remove from the oven and transfer to a wire rack to cool completely.

CHESTNUT BEIGNETS

A *beignet* is a cross between a fritter and a doughnut; in Corsica, these little treats are also called *fritelli*. We mostly associate chestnuts with Christmas, but in Corsica they are on the menu every day of the year – in savoury dishes, cakes or desserts, or ground into flour which is then used for polenta, pastry or breads. These beignets have a lovely sweet biscuit flavour from the chestnut flour and are perfect with a cup of tea.

SERVES 4

175g strong white flour,
  plus extra for dusting
125g chestnut flour
1½ tsp instant (fast-action)
  dried yeast
1 tbsp caster sugar
1 tsp salt
25g butter
1 egg yolk
150ml whole milk
vegetable oil,
  for deep-frying

To serve
runny honey
icing sugar, for dusting

Place the flours in a large mixing bowl and add the yeast, sugar and salt. Using your hands, rub in the butter until it is evenly distributed and the mixture resembles fine breadcrumbs. Make a well in the centre and add the egg yolk. Combine the dry ingredients with the egg, adding enough milk to bring the mixture together to form a soft dough. Using your hands, knead together for a couple of minutes until you have a smooth ball. Transfer to a lightly oiled bowl, cover and leave to prove in a warm place for at least 2 hours or until doubled in size.

On a lightly floured work surface, roll out the dough to around 2cm thick. Cut into diamond shapes, each around 3cm in length.

Fill a large deep heavy-based saucepan with oil to a depth of 4cm and set over a medium heat. Test the oil is hot enough for deep-frying by dropping in a small piece of bread: it should sizzle and brown in 40 seconds. Add the beignets to the hot oil in batches of no more than four or five at a time to ensure they are not touching. Fry for 3–4 minutes, then turn and fry the other side until golden brown. Remove with a slotted spoon to drain on kitchen paper and keep warm while you cook the rest.

To serve, drizzle with a little honey and dust with icing sugar. Eat immediately.

CREMA CATALANA

Crema Catalana is a classic Spanish dessert similar to a French crème brûlée – it's a smooth Spanish custard with a hint of citrus and spice, topped with a hardened caramel. A traditional Catalana is not as rich as a crème brûlée and the Spanish use cinnamon rather than vanilla to flavour the custard. Originally from Catalonia, the dessert is popular throughout Spain and I definitely enjoyed a couple while in Seville and Granada. Although not traditional, you can top with some fresh seasonal fruit, if you like – I like to serve mine with raspberries or figs.

SERVES 4-6

500ml whole milk
pared zest of 1 large
    lemon, pith removed
pared zest of ½ orange,
    pith removed
1 cinnamon stick,
    broken in half
6 egg yolks
60g caster sugar
1½ heaped tbsp cornflour
    (you can use less if
    you prefer a runnier
    consistency)
4–6 tbsp light brown sugar
fresh raspberries and mint
    sprigs, to serve (optional)

Put a heavy-based saucepan over a low–medium heat and add the milk, pared zests and cinnamon stick. Gently bring to the boil. As soon as it begins to boil, remove from the heat and set aside for 20 minutes to allow the flavours to infuse.

Meanwhile, beat or whisk the egg yolks, sugar and cornflour together in a bowl until pale, thick and creamy.

Using a slotted spoon, remove the cinnamon stick and pared zests from the infused milk and place the pan back over a very low heat. Slowly add the egg mixture to the warm milk, whisking continuously for 8–10 minutes until the cream begins to thicken. When the liquid is thick enough to coat the back of a wooden spoon, remove the pan from the heat and pour the mixture into six shallow serving dishes or four ramekins.

Cover the dishes and let cool to room temperature, then transfer to the fridge to chill for a couple of hours.

To serve, sprinkle a layer of brown sugar on top of each dessert and caramelise using a blowtorch or by placing under a hot grill until the sugar bubbles and turns golden brown. Allow the sugar to harden, then serve immediately, scattered with raspberries and fresh mint, if using.

ORANGE CARDAMOM PANNA COTTA WITH SPICED MANDARINS & PISTACHIO CRUMB

Panna cotta is one of Italy's most-loved desserts. It's a delightfully creamy pudding that is elegant enough for a special dinner, but is also surprisingly easy to make. I've added a hint of Middle-Eastern flavour with aromatic orange blossom, a crunchy crumb of pistachio and gently spiced mandarins. Check the packet instructions because you may need more or fewer gelatine sheets depending on the brand. You can easily make this a vegan dessert by using dairy-free milk and cream (such as soya or coconut) and a gelatine substitute, which are all now readily available in supermarkets.

SERVES 4

2 gelatine leaves
250ml double cream
250ml whole milk
30g caster sugar
1 cardamom pod, cracked
1 tsp orange blossom water
(brands vary in strength, so adjust to taste)

For the Spiced Mandarins
1 x 298g tin mandarins in natural juice
1 tbsp runny honey
1 star anise
2 cardamom pods, cracked
1 cinnamon stick, broken in half
juice of ½ lemon, or to taste

For the Pistachio Crumb
35g granulated sugar
sunflower oil, for greasing
30g pistachio nuts

Soak the gelatine leaves in cold water for 10 minutes until soft.

Meanwhile, combine the cream, milk, sugar, cardamom pod and orange blossom water in a heavy-based saucepan over a medium heat and bring just to the boil. Remove from the heat.

Squeeze out the excess water from the gelatine and add to the hot cream mixture. Whisk to dissolve the gelatine, then pass the cream through a sieve into a jug. Pour into four ramekins, leave to cool for 5 minutes, then chill in the fridge for 4 hours until set.

To make the spiced mandarins, set a sieve over a saucepan and drain the juice from the tin into the pan. Set the mandarins aside in a bowl. Add the honey, star anise, cardamom pods and cinnamon stick to the pan and bring to the boil, then remove from the heat and allow to cool and infuse for 30–40 minutes.

Remove the spices from the infused syrup and stir in lemon juice to taste. Pour the syrup over the reserved mandarins and chill in the fridge until ready to serve.

For the pistachio crumb, place the sugar in a saucepan with 1 tablespoon of water. Heat gently over a low heat until the sugar dissolves, then bring to the boil and simmer rapidly until golden.

While the sugar is boiling, brush a baking tray with a little oil and scatter the pistachios over it in an even layer, keeping them close together. As soon as the caramel is golden, remove from the heat, allow the bubbles to subside, then pour the caramel over the nuts. Leave to cool and set.

Place the cooled praline on a board and use a heavy knife to chop it into shards. Place the shards into a food processor and blitz to a coarse crumb – you still want to have a bit of crunch.

When ready to serve, dip the ramekins into warm water to release and tip the panna cotta out onto serving plates. Serve with the spiced mandarins and a sprinkling of pistachio crumb.

PLUM FRANGIPANE TART

This twist on a classic Bakewell tart is an attractive and great-tasting dessert or treat. I love juicy fresh plums and their rich and seductive flavour works perfectly with the velvety almond base. You can add a zesty lemon icing to lift the flavour of the tart if you like – just mix 50g icing sugar with 2 or 3 tablespoons of lemon juice until smooth and then drizzle over the surface of the cooled tart.

SERVES 6-8

For the pastry
200g plain flour, plus
    extra for dusting
2 tbsp icing sugar
100g cold unsalted
    butter, diced
1 medium egg
2–3 tsp cold water

For the frangipane
100g unsalted butter
100g caster sugar
2 large eggs
55g plain flour
70g ground almonds
a drop of almond essence

To assemble
100g plum jam
3–4 plums, stone removed,
    cut into thin wedges

First, make the pastry. Sift the flour and icing sugar into a large bowl. Add the butter and rub it in with your fingertips until the mixture resembles fine breadcrumbs. Make a well in the centre and add the egg and 2 teaspoons of cold water. Stir, combining the dry ingredients into the wet, adding another teaspoon of water if necessary. When the pastry starts to come together, gently knead into a smooth ball. Cover the pastry with clingfilm and chill in the fridge for at least 15 minutes.

Meanwhile, preheat the oven to 200°C/180°C fan/gas 6.

Unwrap the chilled pastry, place on a lightly floured work surface and roll out to about 3mm thick. Line a 23-cm diameter loose-bottomed tart tin with the pastry, leaving a little excess pastry hanging over the edges. Line the pastry case with a sheet of baking parchment and fill with baking beans or raw rice. Bake blind for 12–15 minutes, until the pastry is dry to the touch, then remove the parchment and baking beans and return the pastry case to the oven for a further 5 minutes until it is very lightly coloured. Use a small, sharp knife to trim away the excess pastry from the edges and then leave the pastry case to cool slightly while you prepare the filling.

Reduce the oven temperature to 180°C/160°C fan/gas 4.

To make the frangipane, beat the butter and sugar together in a large bowl until light and fluffy, then beat in the eggs one at a time. Stir in the flour, ground almonds and almond extract.

Spread the jam over the base of the pastry case, then top with the frangipane. Smooth the surface with a spatula or back of a spoon, then push the plum slices onto the surface of the frangipane, arranging them in an attractive pattern.

Bake for 25–30 minutes until the filling is golden and well risen. Leave to cool in the tin before slicing.

SALTED CHOCOLATE & TAHINI BROWNIES

Don't let the name of these brownies put you off – they are sumptuous. Full of the chocolate richness and fudginess you expect from a brownie, with a little of the unexpected from the earthy and nutty tahini and hint of saltiness. Give them a go – they are a real grown-up treat and you won't be disappointed.

MAKES 12

200g good-quality dark chocolate (minimum 60% cocoa solids), broken into small chunks
200g butter, diced
130g caster sugar
130g soft light brown sugar
3 large eggs
170g plain flour
50g chocolate chips
2 tbsp tahini
1 tsp sea salt flakes

Preheat the oven to 200°C/180°C fan/gas 6. Line a 20-cm square baking tin with baking parchment.

Gently melt the chocolate and butter together in a medium saucepan over a low heat, stirring continuously until well mixed, smooth and shiny. Remove from the heat and add the sugars, mixing well until dissolved. Add the eggs and use a hand whisk to beat until smooth, then add the flour and chocolate chips and mix until thoroughly combined.

Pour the mixture into the prepared tin. Dot small spoonfuls of tahini on top and use a skewer to swirl it through the mixture. Sprinkle the sea salt flakes over the top.

Bake for 20–25 minutes until the top is crisp and the middle still has a slight wobble.

Leave to cool in the tin, then place in the fridge to cool completely before cutting into squares.

SEADAS SWEET CHEESE PASTRIES WITH APPLE & PEAR SALAD & THYME HONEY

Seadas or *sebadas* are a delicious Sardinian dessert traditionally eaten at Easter. They are a slightly savoury, crispy fried pastry filled with an oozing lemony cheese filling. When combined with the warm sweet honey, they're truly delightful. A real treat!

MAKES 12

For the pastry
450g semolina flour
    or plain '00' flour,
    plus extra for dusting
2 tsp caster sugar
a pinch of salt
50g butter
200ml warm water,
    or as needed

For the filling
500g Casizolu, pecorino
    or mozzarella, cut
    into small cubes
zest of 2 unwaxed lemons
    (or oranges)
sunflower oil,
    for deep-frying

For the salad
1 apple
1 pear
juice of ½ lemon
½ tsp fresh thyme leaves

To serve
125g good-quality honey
    (I used thyme honey)

First, make the pastry dough. In a large bowl, combine the flour, sugar and salt. Rub in the butter with your fingertips until the mixture resembles breadcrumbs, then slowly add the water, kneading it as you go until you have a dough with a smooth elastic texture. Knead until you have a smooth ball, then cover and let it rest in a warm place for 30 minutes.

Meanwhile, make the filling. Grease or line a baking tray. Melt the cheese in a small saucepan over a low heat. If it starts to separate, you can add a little flour to bring it back together. Once melted, stir in the lemon zest, then pour the mixture out onto the prepared tray. Use the back of a metal spoon or spatula to spread it out to about 5mm thick, then leave to cool completely.

When the filling mixture is cool, use a 5.5-cm round pastry cutter to cut out 12 discs.

On a lightly floured work surface, roll out the pastry dough to around 2–3mm thick. Use a 8.5-cm round pastry cutter to cut out 24 discs. Place a disc of cheese filling in the middle of a disc of pastry, dampen the edge with a touch of water, then top with a second disc of pastry, pressing the edges well with your fingers or a fork to seal. Repeat with the remaining cheese filling and pastry discs until you have 12 filled pastries.

To make the salad, thinly slice the apple and pear, leaving the skins on, and place in a bowl. Mix with the lemon juice and thyme leaves and set aside.

Fill a large deep heavy-based frying pan with oil to a depth of 3cm and set over a medium heat. Test the oil is hot enough for deep-frying by dropping in a small piece of bread: it should sizzle and brown in 40 seconds. Fry the pastries in batches of no more than 3 or 4 at a time until golden on both sides. Remove from the oil with a slotted spoon to drain on kitchen paper and keep warm while you cook the rest.

Serve immediately, drizzled with the honey and with the apple and pear salad on the side.

BAKED CORSICAN CHEESECAKE

This is a really easy, zesty gluten-free Corsican dessert that's a cross between a flan and a baked cheesecake. On the island, they have a local liqueur called 'myrtle eau de vie', made from the berries of the myrtle shrub, which has a very distinct and slightly aromatic flavour. If you can find some, then do use it to add a unique flavour; otherwise, use limoncello for a delicate lemony treat.

SERVES 6–8

butter or vegetable oil,
    for greasing
500g ricotta cheese
    (or brocciu/brousse
    cheese, if you can
    get it)
140g caster sugar
zest of 2 large
    unwaxed lemons
4 eggs
1 tbsp myrtle liqueur/
    eau de vie, limoncello
    or grappa
mixed fresh berries,
    to serve

Preheat the oven to 180°C/160°C fan/gas 4. Lightly grease a 20-cm springform cake tin and line the bottom with baking parchment.

Strain off any excess liquid from the ricotta by placing it in a sieve over a bowl for 20–30 minutes. Once strained, place the cheese in a mixing bowl and break it down using a fork. Add 40g of the sugar and the lemon zest and mix well.

In a separate bowl, use an electric mixer to whisk the eggs with the remaining sugar for 4–6 minutes until pale, fluffy and tripled in volume. Slowly add the egg mixture, a little at a time, to the ricotta mixture, gently folding it in, making sure to keep as much air in the mixture as possible. Do not over-mix. Add the liqueur and gently mix in.

Pour the mixture into the cake tin and bake for 40–45 minutes or until the top is lightly golden and set, but still with a very slight wobble. It will firm up as it cools. Leave to completely cool in the tin before turning out onto a serving plate, then chill before cutting into slices and serving with fresh berries.

FIG TARTE TATIN WITH ORANGE & CINNAMON CREAM

I love a tarte tatin. Glorious sticky caramel with soft fruit and puff pastry…
Mmmm! This is my Eastern-Mediterranean-inspired tart with the luscious flavour
of figs and the delicate warm spice of cinnamon. If you don't have orange blossom
water, you can add Cointreau to the cream for a slight boozy kick.

SERVES 6

zest and juice of
 ½ large orange
1 heaped tsp ground
 cinnamon
10–12 large black figs,
 stems trimmed,
 halved lengthways
1 x 375g pack ready-made
 puff pastry
plain flour, for dusting
100g golden caster sugar
60g cold unsalted
 butter, cubed
25g pistachios, toasted:
 half finely chopped;
 half roughly chopped

**For the Orange and
 Cinnamon Cream**
200ml double cream
1 tbsp icing sugar
½ tsp ground cinnamon
zest of ½ large orange
½ tsp orange blossom
 water, or to taste

Preheat the oven to 200°C/180°C fan/gas 6 and line a baking
tray with baking parchment.

In a large bowl, mix together the orange juice and half of
the ground cinnamon. Add the figs, toss to coat and set aside.

Open out the pastry on a lightly floured surface and cut
out a disc just bigger than your pan (about 25cm diameter).
Place the pastry disc on the lined baking tray and prick all
over with a fork. Chill or freeze while you prepare the topping.

Place a 24-cm heavy ovenproof frying pan, tatin dish or hob-
safe oven dish over a low heat, add the sugar and remaining
cinnamon and gently heat, without stirring, until dissolved.
Increase the heat to medium and cook for 1–2 minutes until
the sugar turns a dark golden caramel colour. Gently swirl the
pan/dish, if necessary but do not stir. Remove from the heat
and gradually add the cubed butter, stirring or whisking
to combine, until the mixture looks like a glossy caramel.
Sprinkle over the finely chopped pistachios and orange zest,
then snugly pack the figs into the caramel, cut-side down.

Place the chilled pastry on top of the pan and use a fork to roughly
tuck in the edges, so that when the tarte is turned out it will
hold in the caramel. With a sharp knife, prick the pastry a couple
of times to allow any steam to escape. Bake for 30–35 minutes
or until the pastry has risen and is golden brown in colour.

Meanwhile, make the spiced cream. Whisk the double cream
with the icing sugar until soft peaks form, then add the
cinnamon, orange zest and orange blossom water to taste.
Whisk gently until combined. Chill until ready to serve.

Remove the tart from the oven and let it rest for 1–2 minutes,
then loosen the edges with a blunt knife. Place a large plate
on top of the pan and, in one swift movement, invert the tarte
onto the plate. Sprinkle with the roughly chopped pistachios.
Cut into slices and serve with a spoonful of the spiced cream.

PEACH & MASCARPONE PAVLOVAS WITH POMEGRANATE CARAMEL SYRUP

'Granada' means 'pomegranate' in Spanish and the fruit is an important symbol of the city. Everywhere you go, you will see images of the fruit – on street signs, statues and even on manhole covers. Spanish peaches are some of the juiciest I've ever eaten, so this dessert is a nod to the fresh fruit of Granada. It's a simple treat that impresses with flavour and presentation. To make it even easier and less time-consuming, you can cheat with shop-bought meringue nests. I won't tell anyone!

SERVES 6

150ml double cream
125g mascarpone
1 tbsp icing sugar
2 tsp sherry or 1 tsp
  vanilla extract
50g pomegranate seeds
2–3 ripe peaches or
  nectarines, stoned
  and thinly sliced
2 tbsp flaked almonds,
  toasted

For the meringues
3 egg whites
a small pinch of salt
175g caster sugar
1 tsp cornflour
½ tsp white wine vinegar

**For the Pomegranate
  Caramel Syrup**
50g pomegranate seeds
juice of ½ orange
3 tbsp caster sugar

First, make the meringues. Preheat the oven to 140°C/120°C fan/gas 1 and line a baking tray with baking parchment.

Place the egg whites in a large clean mixing bowl, add the salt and whisk until firm peaks form. Whisk in the sugar, 1 tablespoon at a time, until you have a thick, glossy meringue, then fold in the cornflour and vinegar until well combined.

Drop six even-sized spoonfuls of the mixture onto the prepared baking tray, spacing them well apart (use two trays if easier), and flatten slightly with the back of a spoon, making a small dip in the centre. Bake for 45 minutes or until crisp, then turn off the oven and leave the meringues inside to cool completely (this prevents them from cracking).

When the meringues have cooled, whisk together the cream, mascarpone and icing sugar until smooth and holding soft peaks. Fold in the sherry or vanilla, then fold in the pomegranate seeds. Use the cream mixture to fill the meringues, then top each with fanned slices of peach and scatter over some toasted almonds.

To make the pomegranate caramel syrup, put the pomegranate seeds into a food processor and blitz. Pass the mixture through a sieve, pressing down with the back of a spoon, until you get a nice red juice. Put the pomegranate juice, orange juice and sugar into a heavy-based saucepan over a low heat, stirring until the sugar dissolves. Increase the heat and bubble for 4 minutes until darker in colour and thickened. As the mixture cooks, don't stir but swirl the pan occasionally so it doesn't burn around the edges. Remove from the heat and spoon a little syrup over each pavlova. Serve immediately.

HAZELNUT & CHOCOLATE CAKE WITH AMARETTO CRÈME FRAÎCHE

This gluten-free cake is light yet deliciously rich with earthy hazelnuts. When paired with the amaretto cream, it makes for an indulgent dessert. Chocolatey, nutty and a little bit boozy – fantastic!

SERVES 8

2 tbsp butter, melted,
  plus extra for greasing
3 medium eggs, separated
150g caster sugar
250g ground hazelnuts
2 tsp gluten-free
  baking power
2 tbsp good-quality
  cocoa powder

**For the Amaretto
Crème Fraîche**
1 x 142ml tub crème fraîche
1–2 tbsp amaretto liqueur,
  to taste
1 tbsp icing sugar

To serve
2 tsp icing sugar mixed
  with 2 tsp cocoa powder
2 tbsp chopped hazelnuts,
  toasted

Preheat the oven to 180°C/ 160°C fan/gas 4. Grease a 20-cm round loose-bottomed cake tin and line the base with baking parchment.

Using an electric hand-mixer, beat the egg yolks with half of the sugar until light, airy and pale in colour. Gently fold in the ground hazelnuts, baking powder and cocoa powder – you will have a thick paste at this stage.

In a separate bowl, whisk the egg whites until they form stiff peaks. Add the remaining sugar, a spoonful at a time, whisking after each addition.

Fold the egg whites, a few spoonfuls at a time, into the yolk mixture, then pour the melted butter around the edge of the bowl and gently fold it in.

Pour the mixture into the prepared cake tin and bake for 30–35 minutes.

Meanwhile, make the amaretto crème fraîche. Whip all the ingredients together until the crème fraîche just holds its shape. Chill until ready to serve.

Remove the cake from the oven and leave to cool in the tin. Once cool, remove from the tin and place on a serving plate, then dust with icing sugar and cocoa powder before slicing. Serve with a good dollop of the amaretto crème fraîche and a sprinkle of toasted chopped hazelnuts.

WALNUT & PISTACHIO BAKLAVA

Said to originate from Istanbul, baklava is a sweet, rich and sticky pastry often eaten as a dessert or an afternoon treat with coffee throughout the Levant regions, extending to the Middle East and North Africa. I tried a few variations on my journey. In Jordan, baklava tends to be lighter on the syrup and is most often made with walnuts, while in Marrakesh they use almonds and/or pistachios and also add floral water. I've chosen a combination of the two.

MAKES 28–32 PIECES

250g walnuts
250g unsalted
   pistachios, shelled
50g granulated sugar
2 tsp ground cinnamon
zest of 1 orange
150g salted butter, melted
1–2 x packs filo pastry
   (you'll need 18 sheets –
   see Note below)

For the syrup
350g golden caster sugar
juice of ½ lemon
1 tbsp runny honey
½ tsp ground cinnamon
1–2 tsp orange
   blossom water

Preheat the oven to 160°C/140°C fan/gas 3.

Spread the nuts over a baking tray and bake for 10–15 minutes until lightly toasted. When cool enough to handle, finely chop or pulse in a food processor. Place the chopped nuts into a bowl and add the sugar, cinnamon and orange zest and mix well. Divide into three equal amounts.

Lay the filo on a clean dry surface. You need 18 sheets, so cut each sheet in half widthways, or large enough to fit a 5cm-deep baking tin. Cover the filo with a damp cloth to prevent it drying out.

Brush the tin with melted butter and lay a sheet of filo on the base. Brush with butter and repeat until you have six layers in the tin. Scatter one-third of the nut mixture on top, then cover with 3 filo sheets, brushing with butter each time. Add another layer of nut mixture and another 3 sheets of buttered filo, then a final layer of nut mixture. Finish with a top layer of 6 buttered filo sheets.

Using a sharp knife, cut the baklava two-thirds of the way through into diamond or square shapes. Brush over any remaining butter, then bake for 55–60 minutes until golden.

When the baklava are almost cooked, make the syrup. Place the sugar and lemon juice into a saucepan along with 200ml water, and cook over a low heat, stirring, until the sugar has dissolved. Add the honey and cinnamon, increase the heat to medium, and bring to the boil. Reduce the heat and simmer for 8–10 minutes until syrupy. Allow to cool before adding the orange blossom water.

Remove the baklava from the oven and slowly pour over the warm syrup, concentrating on the scored lines. Increase the oven temperature to 180°C/160°C fan/gas 4 and return the baklava to the oven for 4–5 minutes. Remove from the oven and leave to cool completely in the tin before cutting fully into pieces.

NOTE: Packs of filo pastry vary in size. To avoid waste, choose a baking tin to suit the size of the sheets. I used 30 x 40-cm sheets and a 30 x 20-cm baking tin, but if yours measure 48 x 25cm, choose a smaller tin 24-cm square (or a larger tin and 2 packs).

WATERMELON, ROSE & POMEGRANATE PARFAIT

Watermelon is popular throughout the Mediterranean and each country
we visited served slices of the cooling fruit as a refreshing end to the meal –
much appreciated after a long, hot day of filming. The pomegranate seeds
here add texture and little bursts of tart sweetness, and the aromatic
fragrance of rosewater lifts the watermelon to another level. This is such
a simple dessert, but it looks beautiful and tastes so summery. Heavenly!

SERVES 4

zest and juice of ½ lemon
2 tbsp very finely chopped
  fresh mint leaves
1 tsp rosewater,
  or more to taste
600g watermelon flesh,
  cut into 2-cm cubes
seeds from 1 pomegranate
1 x 227ml tub double cream
120ml crème fraîche
1 tbsp runny honey
1 tbsp chopped pistachios

Put the lemon juice, chopped mint and ½ teaspoon of
the rosewater into a large bowl and mix together. Add the
watermelon cubes and pomegranate seeds (reserving a few
for garnish) and gently toss. Taste to check if more rosewater
is needed and add a little more if so. Cover and chill until
ready to serve.

In a large bowl, whisk the double cream until stiff peaks
form and briefly set aside.

In a separate bowl, whisk together the crème fraîche, honey,
lemon zest and the remaining ½ teaspoon of rosewater until
smooth. Gently fold the crème fraîche mixture into the whipped
cream until smooth and fluffy. If the cream has lost its height,
gently whisk again. Chill until ready to serve.

Leaving any juice behind in the bowl, divide half of the
watermelon and pomegranate seeds between four serving
glasses, then top with half of the cream. Add another layer of
watermelon and pomegranate, and then a final layer of cream.
Garnish with the reserved pomegranate seeds and chopped
pistachios and serve immediately.

ZINGY LIMONCELLO & STEM GINGER GRANITA

Limoncello, the classic Italian liqueur, is predominantly made in southern Italy but they also make it in Sardinia. We enjoyed a glass or two after a long day's filming, that's for sure! It has an intense lemon flavour and the drink is usually served cold as an after-dinner digestif. It's perfect here in this granita, which is great as a palate cleanser or a refreshing dessert on a hot day. Ginger and lemon is a classic flavour combination and the stem ginger really adds some zing.

SERVES 6

180g caster sugar
zest and juice of 2 lemons
150ml limoncello
50g stem ginger,
    finely chopped

To serve
10 mint leaves, shredded,
    for garnish

Put the caster sugar and 600ml cold water into a saucepan over a medium heat and bring to the boil. Stir until the sugar has dissolved, then add the lemon zest and gently boil for 6–8 minutes until the liquid has reduced slightly. Remove from the heat and leave to cool a little before stirring in the lemon juice, limoncello and stem ginger. Set aside to cool completely.

When cool, pour into one or two shallow freezer-proof containers. Place in the freezer for at least 2 hours, after which time ice crystals should have formed. Fork through the granita to break up any clumps, then place back in the freezer. Repeat this process every 50–60 minutes until the granita is completely frozen with a light and fluffy texture.

To serve, spoon into serving glasses and garnish with the shredded mint.

ORANGE & CINNAMON HOT CHOCOLATE WITH QUICK CINNAMON BISCUIT DIPPERS

The Spanish love their hot chocolate and they serve it thick and rich. This is the ultimate hot chocolate for a special treat and when paired with these quick and easy biscuit dippers it's just heavenly. A little bit naughty, but once in a while we all deserve it.

SERVES 4–6
(MAKES 12 BISCUITS)

For the Quick Cinnamon Biscuit Dippers
50g butter, plus extra for greasing
25g caster sugar
75g self–raising flour, plus extra for dusting
¼ tsp ground cinnamon
zest of ½ orange
2 tsp granulated sugar

For the Orange and Cinnamon Hot Chocolate
570ml whole milk
200g dark chocolate (minimum 60% cocoa solids), roughly chopped
1 tsp cornflour
1 tbsp cold milk
½ tsp ground cinnamon
zest of 1 orange
1½ tbsp sugar (optional, to taste)

To serve
whipped cream (optional)
2 tbsp grated dark chocolate

Start with the biscuit dippers. Preheat the oven to 180°C/160°C fan/gas 4 and lightly grease a baking tray with butter.

Put the butter and sugar into a mixing bowl and cream together with a wooden spoon. Add the flour, cinnamon and orange zest and rub between your fingertips until everything starts to come together. When you can knead the mixture into a ball of dough, turn out onto a lightly floured work surface. Divide into 12 equal pieces and roll each piece into a small sausage, about 1cm thick. Place on the prepared baking tray, spaced well apart, and sprinkle with the granulated sugar. Bake for 10–12 minutes until lightly golden.

Remove from the oven and leave to cool on the tray before serving.

Meanwhile, make the hot chocolate. Place the milk in a saucepan over a low heat and slowly bring to the boil. Remove from the heat, add the chocolate and stir until it has completely melted. Add back to a low heat if needed.

In a small bowl, mix the cornflour with the milk.

Place the pan back over a low–medium heat and pour in two-thirds of the cornflour mixture, stirring continuously until the mixture begins to thicken. If it is still a little thin, add the rest of the cornflour mixture and stir well. Add the cinnamon and orange zest and stir to combine. Taste for sweetness and stir in a little sugar if required.

Pour the hot chocolate into small cups and serve topped with a little whipped cream and sprinkling of grated chocolate, with the biscuit dippers on the side.

MOROCCAN MINT TEA

Tea-making is a crucial part of the Moroccan way of life. Mint tea is offered everywhere you go and is an expression of hospitality, a way of showing respect to your guests. When you look at the method below, you may think it's long, but the process is definitely worth it for a mild sweet tea without any bitterness. Traditionally, mint tea is made in an aluminium or silver teapot, but here I'm using a saucepan to show how easily it can be done at home.

SERVES 4

1 heaped tsp gunpowder
 tea leaves
3 tbsp granulated sugar
8 mint sprigs (spearmint)

Measure out 250ml water into a small saucepan and bring to the boil. Add the tea leaves, remove from the heat and leave to steep for 30 seconds.

Use a tea strainer to strain the infused tea into a bowl, leaving the tea leaves behind in the saucepan. Set the strained liquid aside to use later (this has the essence of the tea).

Add another 250ml water to the saucepan and slowly bring back to the boil. Stir, then strain off and discard the water (this will be bitter and some claim it contains toxins), leaving the tea leaves behind in the pan once again.

Add the sugar and mint to the tea leaves in the saucepan, give everything a stir and then return the original infused tea back to the pan, along with 500ml fresh water. Over a medium heat, bring to a simmer for 5 minutes.

To serve, remove from the heat and pour through a strainer into small heatproof glasses or cups. (Traditionally the first cup of tea is always poured back into the pot and then poured again, as it is said to help circulate the flavours.)

POMPIA PARIDISO COCKTAIL

A pompia is a rare citrus fruit that grows only in the area of Siniscola on Sardinia. The fruit is rather too bitter to eat straight from the tree, but it is used in the preparation of local desserts, sweets and liqueurs. This is a twist on the Paridiso – an Italian cocktail somewhere between a Martini and a Screwdriver. Traditionally, limoncello is used but if you can find Sardinian Pompia liqueur the unique sharp citrus adds a real zing to this refreshing cocktail. It's quite strong, so do add more orange juice and serve over ice if you prefer a longer drink.

SERVES 2

To decorate the glasses
1–2 tbsp coarse
 granulated sugar
1 tbsp Pompia liqueur
 or limoncello

For the cocktail
30ml Pompia liqueur
 or limoncello
90ml vodka (orange-
 flavoured, if you have it)
30ml Campari or Aperol
60ml fresh orange juice
a large handful of ice cubes
2 fresh orange wheels,
 to garnish

First, decorate the glasses. Place the sugar on a flat plate and pour the liqueur into a small saucer. Carefully and gently, dip the rim of each cocktail glass into the liqueur, making sure all the rim is coated. Next, dip the rim of each glass into the sugar until coated all the way round and set aside.

For the cocktail, combine all of the ingredients in a cocktail shaker with ice and shake vigorously to chill. Strain into the cocktail glasses and garnish each with an orange wheel.

EXTRA RECIPES

HOMEMADE LABNEH

Soft labneh is delicious served with olive oil and za'atar. For a firmer cheese to make into balls for marinating in oil with herbs, citrus zest or chilli, drain for more than 12 hours.

½ tsp salt
500g plain thick yoghurt (preferably Greek)

Place a sieve or colander over a bowl and line it with a double layer of clean cheesecloth. Make sure the sieve is 5–10cm from the base of the bowl. Stir the salt into the yoghurt, then pour into the centre of the cloth. Bring the corners of the cloth together and twist to squeeze out the whey. Leave in the sieve over the bowl, cover and put in the fridge to drain for 8–16 hours. The longer you leave the labneh, the firmer it becomes; it also depends on the thickness of the yoghurt used, so do check from time to time. Remove from the cloth and serve immediately or store in an airtight container in the fridge for up to 2 weeks.

FLAVOURED HUMMUS

Jazz up your hummus. Follow the recipe on page 33 and then, after blitzing the chickpeas, add the following ingredients to create a delicious flavoured hummus. Adjust the olive oil and chickpea liquid until you reach the desired consistency.

Roasted Red Pepper Hummus – add 2–3 roasted
    red peppers from a jar, roughly chopped
Creamy Coriander Hummus – add a handful
    of chopped coriander leaves and 2–3 tbsp
    of Greek yoghurt
Spicy Hummus – add ½ tsp cayenne pepper, a good
    pinch of pul biber and serve drizzled with chilli oil
Roasted Beetroot Hummus – add 250g roasted
    beetroot, roughly chopped

AIOLI

A simple Spanish aioli or a garlic mayonnaise is a wonderful thing and is a tasty accompaniment to many dishes in the book. Try with my Moorish Lamb Kebabs, Salt-Cod Fish Balls, Za'atar Schnitzel or just with crispy potatoes!

2 large egg yolks
1 garlic clove, minced
a splash of white wine vinegar
125–150ml olive oil

Whisk the egg yolks in a bowl with the grated garlic and a splash of white wine vinegar. Slowly whisk in the oil until thick. Season with salt. Cover and chill until needed.

YOGHURT WITH CUCUMBER & MINT

This dip is similar to Greek Tzatziki and is a simple mezze that can be served with pitta or used as a cooling accompaniment.

500g Greek yoghurt
2 garlic cloves, grated
1 tbsp fresh mint or dill, finely chopped
    plus extra for garnish or 1 tsp dried mint
juice and zest of ½ lemon
2 tbsp extra-virgin olive oil
1 medium cucumber, de-seeded
    and coarsely grated
sea salt and freshly ground black pepper

In a bowl add the yoghurt, garlic, mint/dill, lemon zest and olive oil. Squeeze any excess liquid from the grated cucumber and pat dry with kitchen paper. Add to the yoghurt and mix well to combine all of the ingredients. Stir in the lemon juice to taste and season. Cover and refrigerate until ready to serve. Serve with a drizzle of olive oil and extra mint or dill for garnish.

STORECUPBOARD ESSENTIALS

Most of the ingredients in the book will be familiar to you, after all Italian, Spanish and Moroccan cuisines are amongst the most popular in the world. However, there are a couple of ingredients which I highly recommend adding to your store cupboard if you don't already have them in.

OLIVE OIL
What is typical for perhaps all Mediterranean countries is the use of olives and olive oil. Of course, the Spanish and Italians hold their own where olive oil is concerned but it is also true that the Middle East and Morocco produces wonderful oils. All have their own unique flavour – Spanish oil is fruity and nutty, Italian is grassy and herbal, Corsican oil is aromatic, complex and nutty, Moroccan is fruity with a hint of almonds and pepper and Jordanian olive oil is aromatic and fruity. Most recipes call for olive oil or extra-virgin olive oil and if it's for drizzling it really is worth getting a decent quality - you want to be able to taste the character of the olives. Don't worry, I don't expect you to buy a different oil from each region.

THYME
Thyme has a warm, earthy and slightly spicy flavour and it is used frequently in Mediterranean and Middle Eastern cooking. It's probably the herb I use most in the book. It's a versatile herb that pairs well with most meats, fish and vegetables and also complements other herbs and spices such as allspice, chilli, garlic and rosemary. I've mostly used fresh thyme, but you can substitute for dried if easier. As a general rule use half of the stated amount of fresh to dried.

HERBES DE PROVENCE
Although I didn't visit mainland France there are a few French influenced recipes in the book from the island of Corsica. The island is covered in a blanket of fresh herbs and flora used in the local cooking and many aren't available off the island. Herbes de Provence usually contains basil, fennel, marjoram, parsley, rosemary, tarragon and thyme. By using this I hope I've come close to recreating the unique flavours of the Corsican cuisine.

CUMIN
Another of the spices used frequently throughout the book whether as a ground powder or in seed form toasted and then crushed in a pestle and mortar. Originating from the Levant, cumin is a widely used spice - after pepper it's said to be the most popular spice in the world. It's a member of the parsley family and has an earthy, warm flavour with slightly bitter undertones. It's great for adding depth to curries and stews but also for lifting the flavour of vegetables such as beetroot or carrot.

PAPRIKA
A bright red pepper from Spain called pimentón. Paprika comes in various strengths from sweet (*dulce*) to spicy (*picante*). The smoked variety is unique to Spain and the peppers have been dried over oak fires. I've mostly used the La Chinata brand from the La Vera region of Spain which is readily available in supermarkets at an affordable price. It's worth getting a sweet and a hot smoked if you can because they both have their uses.

SAFFRON
Saffron, from the dried stigma of a certain type of crocus flower, is one of the most expensive spices in the world. Luckily you only need a little at a time because the flavour really is quite potent. The flavour of saffron is often described as musty and hay-like with metallic honey notes. If used too liberally, however, it can have a medicinal tang so do use sparingly.

ALEPPO PEPPER/PUL BIBER
A ground red chilli pepper from Turkey and Syria and popular in Eastern Mediterranean cooking. It has a moderate heat and a lovely fruity and smoky cumin taste. If you can't find it then you can use cayenne or dried chilli flakes, but these can be hotter so adjust according to taste.

SUMAC
Originating from the Middle East and Southern Italy this is a red powdered spice made from the berries of the sumac bush. It's tangy, fruity and adds an exotic lemony note to dishes.

NIGELLA SEEDS
Tiny black seeds also known as black cumin. They're one of the oldest spices known to have been used in cooking. Used in Middle-Eastern and also Indian cooking to add a slightly bitter, nutty onion flavour to breads, salads and curries. You can find them in supermarkets or world food stores.

RAS EL HANOUT
A dry spice blend widely used in Moroccan cooking. It usually contains between 10 and 12 spices, but it can contain up to 27 different spices. I was sold a blend in the souks of Marrakesh that was said to contain 35! Typically, it contains cardamom, nutmeg, cinnamon, cumin and chilli.

BAHARAT

A dry spice blend used across the Middle East, the Levant and North Africa. Traditionally it contains cumin, cardamom, cinnamon, coriander, caraway, black pepper, nutmeg and paprika but each region has its own version and it can also contain allspice and cloves. It's great for marinating meat and also works well with vegetables and pulses (see my Carrot, Courgette & Broad Bean Baharat Burgers, page 54).

ZA'ATAR OR ZAHTAR

A dry spice mix used in the Levant and the Middle East. The three main ingredients are sesame seeds, thyme and sumac but it can also contain other herbs and spices. It's usually used to flavour meats and fish but also works well in sauces and as a seasoning. Try adding to your favourite olive oil as a dip for fresh bread or pitta.

PRESERVED LEMONS

Lemons which have been pickled in salt have a zingy, sweet taste that's quite unique. They add a punchy citrus kick to dishes and are used frequently in Moroccan and Middle Eastern cuisine. Great for adding to traybakes, tagines, dressings, marinades and salads.

TAHINI

A thick Middle-Eastern paste made from crushed sesame seeds which is a staple of Middle-Eastern and Eastern-Mediterranean cooking. It's used to make hummus and is also great when used in salad dressings and dips. Tahini from the Middle East is runnier than the Cypriot version we mostly get here in the UK, so when following recipes, if it looks too thick, stir in a little water until you reach the consitency that you want. For something a little different try my Salted Chocolate and Tahini Brownies (see page 189).

HARISSA

You've probably already come across this spicy red pepper paste from North Africa – it's become very popular in recent years. Made from chillies, garlic and saffron with a blend of spices such as cumin and cayenne, it's great for adding a kick to stews, tagines and marinades. Rose harissa contains rose petals and has a lovely aromatic flavour.

POMEGRANATE AND POMEGRANATE MOLASSES

Pomegranates feature in the cuisine of many Mediterranean countries and they have a unique sweet tart flavour. Pomegranate molasses is a rich tangy syrup made from the fruit and it's an essential ingredient in Middle Eastern cooking. It adds a wonderful sweet and sour note to dishes and is great in marinades and dressings.

DATES AND DATE MOLASSES

Dates are one of the oldest known cultivated fruits and they are mostly grown in Israel and North Africa. Medjool dates, from Morocco are probably the sweetest with a rich caramel taste and chewy texture. They're delicious in salads. Date molasses is a rich sticky syrup used as a sweetener in Middle Eastern cooking. It can now be found in most supermarkets and is great in salad dressings, marinades or try it drizzled on thick yoghurt or ice-cream.

ORANGE BLOSSOM WATER AND ROSE WATER

These aromatic and floral waters are popular ingredients in Middle-Eastern and North-African cuisine and are used in both savoury and sweet dishes. They have an intense flavour and so need to be used with care, but they can add a unique and exotic twist to your cooking. They do come in different strengths so check your label before using.

I've used a concentrated essence (such as Neilsen-Massey or Steenbergs) so do adjust according to taste and strength.

NUTS AND SEEDS

Nuts and seeds are used in Mediterranean cooking to add texture and flavouring, and I always make sure I have plenty in the kitchen cupboard. Not only do they make a healthy snack they're great for sauces, salads and adding texture to sweet and savoury dishes. Pine nuts are popular in Italian, Spanish and Middle Eastern cooking and they are great for adding a sweet buttery, nutty taste and a unique texture to rice and salads.

TINNED CHERRY TOMATOES

Tinned tomatoes are perhaps an obvious store cupboard ingredient, but they are important when cooking Mediterranean food. They range in price and mostly you get what you pay for, so do try and get the best you can. Tinned cherry tomatoes are slightly more expensive, but for certain recipes they are worth getting for a sweeter and more textured sauce.

CITRUS

Although not a store cupboard ingredient I just wanted to mention the importance of citrus fruits – an essential ingredient in Mediterranean cuisine. Fresh orange and lemon in particular are used to freshen up and give balance to sweet and savoury dishes throughout the Med. I can't imagine cooking without a squeeze of fresh lemon, orange or lime.

SHERRY VINEGAR

Made from sherry, this specialty vinegar from Spain has a complex, nutty, caramel flavour that adds a bittersweet note. You can use red wine vinegar instead, although in salad dressings you may need a pinch of sugar for sweetness.

INDEX

ACKNOWLEDGEMENTS

It's been such a blast! What an amazing trip around the Mediterranean with a great team from Rock Oyster Media – Claire, Bridget, Emma, Rob, Jonny, Craig, Matt, Matt H, Flick – a big thank you and hugs to you all. With special thanks to the ever-fabulous David Nottage and, of course, ITV. Thank you to all at Penguin Random House and Ebury for making this book happen when we had a crazy deadline to meet. My publisher Lizzy and editor Lisa, you've been great. Thanks to Dan for his beautiful photography and to food stylist Bianca, props stylist Tamzin and designers Alex and Emma – the book looks gorgeous because of you guys. Thanks to Claire Bassano for all your organisation on location and for speed-testing recipes when back at home. To my wonderful family, friends and Bobby dog, thank you as always for your love and support. Last but not least, thank you to my family at JHA who are always there for me – Jerry, Sarah, Julie and, of course, Charlotte who has been at my beck and call 24/7... I couldn't have done it without you. Love, Ainsley xxx